ORGANIC GARDENING
FOR BEGINNERS

ORGANIC GARDENING

FOR BEGINNERS

AN ECO-FRIENDLY GUIDE
TO GROWING VEGETABLES,
FRUITS, AND HERBS

LISA LOMBARDO

ROCKRIDGE
PRESS

For general information on our other products and services or to obtain technical support, please contact our Customer Care Department within the United States at (866) 744-2665, or outside the United States at (510) 253-0500.

Rockridge Press publishes its books in a variety of electronic and print formats. Some content that appears in print may not be available in electronic books, and vice versa.

TRADEMARKS: Rockridge Press and the Rockridge Press logo are trademarks or registered trademarks of Callisto Media Inc. and/or its affiliates, in the United States and other countries, and may not be used without written permission. All other trademarks are the property of their respective owners. Rockridge Press is not associated with any product or vendor mentioned in this book.

Interior and Cover Designer: Jennifer Hsu
Art Producer: Sue Bischofberger
Editor: Gurvinder Singh Gandu
Production Manager: Holly Haydash
Production Editor: Melissa Edeburn

Illustration © 2021 Enya Todd. USDA Plant Hardiness Zone Map, 2012, courtesy of Agricultural Research Service, U.S. Department of Agriculture. Accessed from https://planthardiness.ars.usda .gov/.

All photography used under license from shutterstock.com and iStockphoto.com. Author photo courtesy of Tom Lombardo.

ISBN: Print 978-1-64876-964-1
eBook 978-1-64876-965-8

R0

TO MY DAD FOR RAISING ME AS A GARDENER AND TO MY
MOM FOR TEACHING ME TO PRESERVE THE HARVEST.

CONTENTS

→

INTRODUCTION

In a modest suburban backyard in the late 1960s, a rugged man showed his little girls how to work the soil and sow bean seeds. He patted the black earth and watered the tiny garden.

That guy was my dad, and he instilled in me an undying love of gardening and the natural world. The almost magical appearance of pale green seedlings in spring still fills me with a sense of wonder and well-being.

We moved from the suburbs to our family homestead the summer before I started first grade. Our garden grew in size and produced an abundance of vegetables for freshly prepared meals. Mom worked tirelessly in summer, canning and freezing corn, beans, and tomatoes, all the while teaching us self-reliance skills for the future. Although we were never wealthy, we always had plenty of homegrown food on our table.

Over the years, I've lived in urban apartments and suburban homes, raising food wherever I found space. I joined a community garden, turned flower beds into edible landscaping, and planted dwarf fruit trees. When we moved to our one-acre homestead, I expanded my garden to grow plenty of vegetables, herbs, and fruit for fresh use in summer, plus extra for canning, dehydrating, and freezing.

An increasing number of people are worried about having access to healthy foods, promoting sustainability, and creating a safe outdoor space around their home. One of the best ways to alleviate these concerns is by gardening organically to produce food, provide wildlife habitat, and add natural beauty to the surroundings.

Growing your own organic vegetables, herbs, and fruits is a great way to save money, reduce your carbon footprint, and provide nutrient-dense food for your meals. Purchasing organic produce from the grocery store can be hard on the average family budget, and nutritional content degrades soon after fruits and vegetables are picked. Cut out the middleman and grow varieties known for their delicious flavor rather than their shipping qualities. Use homemade insect control and start your own seeds to reduce your grocery bill and household waste and provide a safe ecosystem in your own backyard.

By converting a section of your resource-hungry lawn into productive garden beds and native plants, you can raise food for your family and for birds, butterflies, bees, and other wild creatures at the same time. You don't need a large space for a garden, and in the following chapters you'll learn how to get the most out of the space you have. You'll also learn how to check the health of your soil and increase its productivity.

In chapter 6, I've included information on how to choose and raise a variety of common food crops. You'll also find plenty of resources to help you attract beneficial creatures to your garden and create an inviting and peaceful space. Additionally, a glossary at the back of the book (page 115) is helpful as a quick reference.

The benefits of gardening organically are immense, and many people switch to this natural means of raising produce for a variety of reasons. If you wish to grow healthy foods, decrease your carbon footprint, or turn your backyard into a natural ecosystem, you'll find that organic gardening is the best way to achieve your goals.

In this book, I cover the basics of how to raise food organically for your own use. If you wish to sell organic produce, you'll need to research current regulations and complete the steps necessary for organic certification. See the Resources (page 118) for more information.

So, get ready to dig in and make your world a better place.

CHAPTER 1

GROWING A NATURALLY HEALTHY GARDEN

Raising organic vegetables, herbs, and fruits is one of the most basic activities known to humans. The production of food to fuel your body might start as a project to save money or reduce the toxins you consume or simply as a way for you to enjoy eating the freshest foods available. Whatever your impetus, you are not the only one to benefit from your garden. The wildlife and people around you will also enjoy the beauty and diversity you create.

Raising a truly organic garden involves much more than planting a tomato seedling and growing it without artificial chemicals. If we care enough about our health to plant a garden and raise our own food without toxins, then we probably also care about the well-being of our planet. Clean drinking water, healthy soil, and habitat for wild creatures are just a few benefits of gardening organically.

WHAT DOES ORGANIC MEAN?

At its most basic definition, organic gardening is the act of growing plants without the use of artificial fertilizers or pesticides. Purchasing organic produce helps support a less toxic industry than that of conventionally grown food because commercial organic growers must abide by strict regulations concerning the sprays and fertilizers used. However, large-scale commercial organic growers often practice monoculture—raising fields of all one crop that require large quantities of water, fuel, and approved fertilizers and pesticides—instead of polyculture, which increases biodiversity and improves soil health.

The home organic gardener can do much more to benefit their wallet, health, and the environment. Raising vegetables, herbs, and fruits at home in small-scale plantings allows a reliance entirely on natural methods. Rotating crops, feeding the soil, and planting a diversity of plants can deter many pests and help prevent disease.

In the 1970s, Bill Mollison and David Holmgren developed the concept of "permaculture" to mean cultivated environments that mimic natural ecosystems in terms of diversity, stability, and resilience. Organic gardeners can create a permaculture haven in their own backyards with small trees and shrubs that provide fruit, compost, and habitat for wildlife. With their deep roots, trees draw on nutrients unavailable to most vegetables and herbs. Their leaves provide free mulch and fertilizer for the garden, enriching the soil and feeding microbes. Birds, beneficial insects, and other creatures are attracted to take up residence in such a diverse landscape. Many of these creatures increase harvest yields by pollinating crops and feasting on pests.

There are many rewards for the gardener who lives in tune with nature instead of reaching for a quick fix from pesticides or synthetic fertilizers. The remainder of this chapter takes a look at the basics of organic gardening at home.

THE ROOT OF A PRODUCTIVE GARDEN: GOOD SOIL

Loose, rich soil that is full of microbes and organic matter is the stuff organic gardeners dream of. However, many people are unaware of just how important healthy soil is for a successful harvest. The secret lies in the symbiotic relationship between plants and the beneficial microbes living in the soil.

Countless microorganisms, insects, fungi, and other life-forms live in the ground beneath our feet. These tiny creatures break down organic matter into more easily used nutrients that plant roots absorb and that fuel growth.

Plants raised with synthetic fertilizers and pesticides have poorly developed root systems with reduced root hair growth, limiting their ability to take up water and nutrients. These chemicals greatly reduce the beneficial soilborne bacteria populations that plants rely on.

On the flip side, when we choose organic methods of feeding crops and soil life, plants grow extensive root systems with a multitude of root hairs. In this sort of healthy system, plant roots excrete carbohydrates that feed microbes, which in turn flock to the rhizosphere, the soil layer that surrounds the surface of the roots. Here, the microbes work symbiotically with plants to increase the absorption of nutrients and help protect their host from disease.

Even gardeners who find that their soil is devoid of insect and microbial life can create mounds of new humus. Adding compost and amending the soil increases soilborne life and fuels healthy plant growth.

We'll dig deeper into the composition, aeration, and enrichment of your garden soil to lay the foundation for healthy plant growth in chapter 3. You'll also learn the basics of composting, so you can create your own soil amendments for boosting overall soil and plant health.

NO PESTICIDES, NO PROBLEM

One of the most common reasons people begin an organic garden is to reduce their exposure to toxins. You'll be happy to hear that it's entirely possible to grow delicious food without synthetic chemicals such as fertilizers, insecticides, and herbicides. However, it involves more than just replacing these products with their organic counterparts. You'll need to take a more holistic approach to tending a garden.

Natural methods such as companion planting, crop rotation, and composting can increase soil fertility and boost plant health. Healthy crops aren't as susceptible to pests and disease because they are under less stress. To further reduce pest problems, include plenty of flowers, herbs, and trees that attract beneficial insects and birds and provide them with a natural habitat. Add toad houses, bird baths, and other perches for birds throughout your yard. These creatures happily gobble up cabbage worms and other "bad guys."

Choosing disease-resistant plant varieties that are adapted to your particular climate as well as picking out a garden spot according to individual plant needs will further increase yields. By providing the best growing conditions for the right plant(s), you'll also reduce the need for pesticides.

You'll still need to carefully monitor your vegetables and fruits for signs of disease or insect damage. As soon as a problem arises, deal with it quickly and apply treatments only to affected plants, to reduce potential damage to beneficial organisms. We'll discuss what problems to watch for and which organic control methods are safe to use in chapter 5.

DIVERSITY SUPPORTS GARDEN HEALTH

Mapping out a garden plan can be a bit overwhelming when you take into consideration crop rotation and companion planting. For this reason, many gardeners just till up the garden, stake out rows and walking paths, and plant crops the way their grandparents did, using a single plant variety.

Although planting in this familiar way may simplify your garden plans, the reasons to mix it up are numerous. For example, several rows of a single type of crop, say beans, side by side will draw bean beetles in for a feast, whereas planting different crops in every other row will confuse pests and reduce chances of serious infestation.

Some plants even deter pests or increase soil fertility for their neighbors, and other plants attract beneficial insects that pollinate flowers or prey on pests in your garden. Interplanting nitrogen-fixing legumes with corn and other heavy feeders is a great way to increase production with less fertilizer. There are also a number of plants that contain natural chemicals that repel pests from the surrounding crops. Put the power of beneficial plant combinations to work in your garden by planting cabbage with garlic and beans with corn, for example.

Protect your garden further with plants that increase soil health, such as legumes and green manure crops. Evidence suggests that bacteria, fungi, and other soil dwellers have an important role to play in protecting plants from pathogens and insects, not only in the root zone but aboveground as well. The discussion in chapter 3 devoted to that glorious garden soil provides more detail.

THE EDIBLE GARDEN AS PART OF A LARGER ECOSYSTEM

In nature, many species of plants, animals, fungi, and other organisms coexist in a complex cycle of life. Plants lay the foundation of this food web by using sunlight, carbon dioxide, and nutrients from the soil to manufacture carbohydrates, the food that fuels all other life, including our own. Before humans began altering ecosystems by planting ever larger fields of crops, people grew much of their own food on small homesteads.

These days the typical family home is surrounded by plants chosen for their looks rather than their nutritional value. We've replaced vegetable gardens and fruit trees with lawns and foundation shrubs. Mowing, watering, fertilizing, and spraying herbicides on our lawns wastes time and money, kills pollinators, and pollutes the air and waterways. If you replace part of your lawn with a vegetable garden and native plants, you'll help reduce pollution, waste less water, and increase your self-reliance with homegrown food.

Consider planting edible flowers and herbs that feed parasitic wasps, ladybugs, and green lacewings and then watch these beneficial insects work tirelessly to rid your plants of tomato hornworms or aphids. Learn which insects are helpful and which are the enemies of your garden. Check out chapter 5 for more information about some common pests and their natural predators; you don't want to handpick the good guys. Surround yourself with a more natural ecosystem and you—and your garden—will thrive.

LET'S GET PLANNING

It's pretty exciting to think about digging into your soil and planting up some herb and vegetable beds. Before you get your hands dirty, though, it's important to make a plan. Take notes about your growing conditions. Determine which plants do well in your area and which vegetables and fruits you want to grow. Jot down the plants you wish to include for improving soil, attracting beneficial insects, or providing organic food for your table. Start a garden journal to track your experiences and inspirations as you read through the upcoming chapters and begin planning your future garden.

CHAPTER 2

HOW DOES YOUR GARDEN GROW?

When most people think of a garden, they envision neat rows of vegetables. However, a single-row garden layout doesn't make the most efficient use of space, nutrients, or time. Plus, not every home gardener has enough land to plant a space-hungry single-row garden.

For very small spaces, your best choice might be a container garden on a sunny patio. If your soil is poor, consider implementing the sheet mulching method or a raised-bed garden. Space-saving ideas include using a biointensive garden or wide-row garden for in-ground, planting in a square-foot system, or raising vegetables vertically. If you have trouble bending down to pull weeds and pick vegetables, a raised-bed garden, such as a keyhole (a circular raised bed with a narrow, wedge-shape path to a central composting system), could work well for you. As we go into a bit more detail in this chapter, consider which of these methods might best suit your specific needs.

GARDEN SETUPS AND LANDSCAPING CHOICES

CONTAINER GARDENS

Raising plants in containers is a great way to increase your gardening space and take advantage of a sunny deck or rooftop. Containers should have drainage holes to prevent root rot and a saucer to catch run-off water. Containers made from recycled plastic or another waterproof material will reduce moisture loss in sunny locations. Grow bags (breathable polypropylene fabric bags filled with potting soil) are another fantastic option for raising vegetables and herbs. If planning a container garden on a rooftop or terrace, bear in mind that containers + soil + plants + water can get heavy.

Use a quality potting soil mix and follow these steps for planting:

» Place gravel in the bottom of the pot to improve drainage.

» Add potting soil.

» Plant seedlings and gently tamp down the soil to remove air pockets.

» Water thoroughly and protect from direct sun until the plants become acclimated.

Best Choices for Vegetable Container Gardens

Many crops work well in containers, including species that are naturally compact or space-saving varieties such as miniature carrots, baby beets, patio tomatoes, and even bush pumpkins. You can raise strawberries, dwarf blueberries, and miniature fruit trees (including citrus) in pots with a bit of extra care. Protect perennial plants from temperature extremes and bring tropical fruits indoors during cold weather. Include herbs or edible flowers to attract pollinators.

Here are a few suitable plant varieties for growing in containers:

Apple: Babe Dwarf and Garden Delicious (plant both for pollination)

Basil: Fino Verde

Beet: Early Wonder

Blueberry: Top Hat

Carrot: Thumbelina

Cherry: Compact Stella (self-pollinating)

Chives: Common Chives or Garlic Chives

Cilantro: Long-standing (bolt resistant)

Citrus: Dwarf Dancy Tangerine or Dwarf Valencia Orange (self-pollinating)

Corn: Golden Miniature

Cucumber: Bush Whopper

Dill: Compatto

Eggplant: Early Black Egg

Kale: Prizm

Lettuce: Tom Thumb

Melon: Green Machine

Peach: Bonanza Miniature (self-pollinating)

Pepper: Baby Belle

Potato: Lady Finger

Pumpkin: Wee Be Little

Spinach: Space

Strawberry: Seascape

Summer squash: Balmoral

Swiss chard: Barese

Tomato: Patio

Winter squash: Jersey Golden Acorn

IN-GROUND GARDENS

Many gardeners choose a traditional in-ground garden to raise food at home. If you have a sunny spot with decent soil and good drainage, consider switching a section of your lawn to an in-ground garden. In windy, dry, or hot climates, the ground will stay cooler and moisture won't evaporate as quickly compared with raised beds or containers. As an added bonus, start-up costs of planting directly into your in-ground garden are usually minimal. Among the planting styles to consider are biointensive single-row or wide-row gardens.

BIOINTENSIVE GARDENS

The biointensive method focuses on building soil fertility and successive plantings. To create a biointensive garden, begin by double-digging compacted soil or simply turning over already loose and friable (easily crumbled) soil. If your climate is cold and wet, the beds may be slightly raised by mounding the soil and leveling them with a garden rake. This style of raised bed uses no lumber or other materials to hold the soil in place. In hot, dry climates, the garden beds are slightly sunken to retain moisture. In any case, each bed is planted into the native soil and amended generously with compost. Mulch is applied between plants to reduce weeds and feed the soil. Every time a crop is harvested, more compost is added to increase soil fertility and a new crop is planted.

SINGLE-ROW GARDENS

A single-row garden is laid out in rows that are one plant wide with walking paths between rows. This design makes envisioning your garden layout easy but requires the most space and leaves a great deal of soil open for weeds to fill in.

WIDE-ROW GARDENS

The wide-row method allows gardeners to increase their harvests by reducing the amount of space dedicated to walking paths. Unlike the single-row system, in which the width of the row depends entirely on how large each crop grows, a wide-row system dedicates about 4 feet for the width of each row or bed. The largest crops may be planted down the center and allowed to fill in the row. Medium-size crops, such as cabbage or tomatoes, are planted in a double row with 1 to 1½ feet between the plants and a walking path down each side of the double row. Spinach, leaf lettuce, and other small plants are usually sown by broadcasting (sprinkling the seeds across the entire wide row) to fill in the space.

By reducing the number of paths and spacing the plants closely, you can raise more crops in your available space, use less water and fertilizer, and reduce weed growth. Mulching the paths further reduces maintenance and increases soil fertility.

LASAGNA GARDENS AND SHEET MULCHING

Lasagna gardening refers to building plant beds with layers of brown and green matter that break down into compost as your plants grow (see page 28). To build a lasagna garden, start by loosening up the soil with a garden fork, covering it with a layer of cardboard or newspaper, then layering brown materials (straw, leaves, etc.) 3 inches thick, alternating with green materials (composted manure, kitchen waste, etc.) 1 inch thick, watering well, then topping off with 2 to 4 inches of soil.

Seeds or seedlings are planted in the soil and may need extra irrigation until the layers fully compost. This method is a wonderful way to improve fertility, start a new garden bed easily, and actually create new soil.

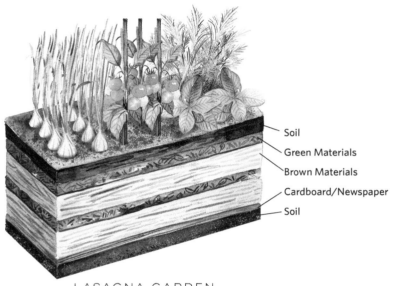

Soil
Green Materials
Brown Materials
Cardboard/Newspaper
Soil

LASAGNA GARDEN

Sheet mulching is basically the same idea; however, you'll cover the soil with cardboard, then add layers of mulch and allow them to break down. The following year, this bed will be ready to plant.

RAISED-BED GARDENS

For gardeners dealing with poor or wet soils, a raised-bed system may be a good option. In this method, a raised structure is built or purchased and filled with soil or a potting mix. Raised beds warm up faster in spring and don't freeze as quickly in fall. In hot, dry climates it's usually better to plant at ground level or in a sunken garden to keep roots cool and reduce moisture loss.

For gardeners with mobility issues, a raised-bed system could make tending vegetables easier. There are also "table"-style gardens, which resemble a cross between a raised bed and a container garden, that allow people in wheelchairs to grow vegetables independently.

When planning a raised-bed garden, allow enough space to walk around the beds, and don't make the beds more than 3 to 4 feet wide, so you can reach the center. Determine the layout of your beds, build the sides, and line the bottom with cardboard or newspaper to help kill grass before adding soil. Consider repurposing old bricks instead of purchasing lumber for the sides. For another sustainable option, consider raised-bed kits made from recycled plastic, available from some garden supply companies.

A keyhole garden is basically a circular raised bed with a central compost bin. This type of garden works well for heavy feeders such as greens and herbs. The compost in the center leaches nutrients into the soil throughout the growing season and may be worked into the bed at the end of the season.

When designing a keyhole garden, don't make the circle so large

KEYHOLE GARDEN

that you aren't able to reach the center of the bed. Keep in mind that the compost bin in the center is key to establishing a healthy soil ecosystem, so this feature shouldn't be eliminated. Another "key" feature of this type of garden is that the path makes it easy to turn your compost and work it into the bed.

Some newer keyhole-garden kits are basically a U-shape raised bed with no composting system included. You could customize such a kit by adding your own compost bin to increase the soil fertility. However, the circular design of the original keyhole-garden layout is designed around the compost pile and makes it easier to distribute the nutrients throughout the bed.

SQUARE-FOOT GARDENS

Square-foot gardening combines a raised-bed system with custom spacing requirements for different crops. A bed is built and filled with equal parts organic compost, vermiculite (a heat-treated mineral that is lightweight and absorbent) or fine bark mulch, and coconut coir or peat moss (we'll discuss why peat moss isn't a sustainable choice in chapter 3; see page 26). A 1-foot-by-1-foot grid is laid out over the bed to guide your planting.

Large plants (such as zucchini or tomatoes) are generally planted in a 2-foot-by-2-foot square (or larger), and smaller crops such as scallions or spinach are planted in a grid of nine plants in a 1-foot-by-1-foot space. Each plant is given enough room to reach maturity without leaving extra space where weeds can fill in and compete with crops.

This compact planting scenario requires less maintenance compared to a traditional single-row system. The "soil" mixture is friable, is great for plant roots, and retains moisture without causing root rot. Fertilizer runoff into paths between rows is no longer an issue when planting intensively. In addition, this system is great for setting up an "instant garden" when you wish to get started quickly.

STRAW-BALE GARDENS

Another option for an easy planting space is a straw-bale garden. In this method, straw bales are placed in a sunny spot and soaked with water several weeks before planting, to begin breaking them down. Situate the bales with the cut-end facing up and remove enough straw from the center of the top of the bale to create a shallow trench. Fill the trench with soil and plant with seeds or seedlings. Keep the straw well watered to speed up decomposition and keep plants hydrated. The rotting straw will nourish your plantings and makes a great soil amendment.

VERTICAL GARDENS AND VERTICAL STACKING

Gardeners with limited space can produce more food by "growing up." The simplest way to make use of vertical space is by training crops on a trellis or arbor instead of letting them sprawl. Vertical gardens are great for such crops as cucumbers, pole beans, and grapes.

You can also raise food in a vertical living wall planter. In this twist on container gardening, a planter system is securely attached to a sturdy wall, filled with potting mix, fitted with an irrigation system, then planted. Creating your own from an already designed plan is an option, or you can purchase one that's ready-made.

Consider this method for small varieties of herbs and salad greens, or choose plants that grow well in a hanging planter, such as strawberries.

Vertical stacking is another technique in which plants with different heights and light requirements are raised together to make better use of space. Tall plants that need full sun work well with shorter, shade-tolerant crops that cover the soil and help reduce weed growth. Some vertical stacking combinations that work well include:

VERTICAL GARDEN

» sweet corn and pumpkins

» sunflowers and lettuce

» tomatoes and spinach

In another vertical-stacking method, a tiered planter provides space to raise vegetables, herbs, and strawberries. Choices include strawberry pots with planting holes in the sides, planters with stepped planting boxes, or tiers of window box–style planters on metal racks.

EDIBLE LANDSCAPING

If you're having trouble working a vegetable garden into your backyard, consider adding edible crops to your decorative landscaping. In addition to creating a lovely and delicious landscape, you'll also provide a diversity of plants to attract beneficial insects. Choose colorful salad greens, herbs, and pretty vegetables and fruits to dress up your landscape as well as your dinner plate. Here are some fantastic choices for edible crops that will look right at home in a flower bed:

» Artichoke

» Bright Lights Swiss chard

» Cayenne pepper

» Cherry tomato

- » Chives
- » Freckles lettuce
- » Opal basil
- » Red Russian kale
- » Scarlet runner bean
- » Seascape strawberry
- » Variegated sage

Other options include blueberry bushes, dwarf fruit trees, and a host of perennial and annual herbs, vegetables, and fruits. Check to see which plants are suitable for your growing conditions, and be sure to include a variety of different heights, textures, colors, and blooms that provide visual interest as well as food for your table (not to mention the butterflies, bees, and birds you wish to attract to your garden).

PICKING THE METHOD THAT WORKS FOR YOU

Given the many different gardening methods to consider, deciding which one is best for you might feel a little overwhelming. Start by setting the location of your new garden, assessing your growing conditions, and determining how much space you can dedicate to growing food. Think, too, about how much time you have to set up and maintain your garden.

Additionally, what are your gardening goals? Which crops do you enjoy eating and how much of each can you put to use? There's a lot to think about, so let's dig in!

HOW MUCH SPACE DO YOU HAVE?

You'll need to take a survey of your property to determine the best location for the fruits, herbs, and vegetables you wish to plant. Having a large, sunny garden space is ideal; however, in the absence of this space sometimes edible plantings must be worked into shady spots or around other complications.

If you have a small yard, consider spaces around your patio, in the foundation plantings around the home, and between the sidewalk and street as potential planting areas. Perhaps there is a community garden nearby where you may rent a space. When planning, be sure to take into account the mature size of trees and shrubs, and consider adding a bed for shade-tolerant crops such as lettuce, peas, spinach, and beets.

Siting and Sizing Your Garden

Start your eco-friendly garden out right by selecting the best location and making good use of what you already have. Here are some handy tips:

» Choose a spot with 6+ hours of sun a day.
» Site your garden near the home and a faucet for easy maintenance.
» Check soil health, structure, and drainage (see chapter 3).
» Avoid underground utilities or septic fields.

Keep in mind that replacing some of your lawn with a garden can increase biodiversity and reduce the time and gas needed to mow. Alternatively, consider growing food in containers on a sunny deck, rooftop, or balcony. Raised beds are a great option for an area with poor drainage or rocky soil. Many edible plants are attractive enough to tuck into a flower bed if you have a small lot.

Another consideration is how much space to plan for your garden. The answer depends on the amount of food you need and which crops you'll grow. One bed of about 12 square feet should be plenty for a single person. For a family of four to eat fresh produce in season and preserve some for winter, you may need to cultivate 96 square feet, or more. Some vegetables need a lot of space (e.g., winter squash and pumpkins), whereas other crops produce an abundance of food in a small space (e.g., tomatoes and pole beans). Use the "My Organic Garden Worksheet" (page 38) to make a list of the crops you wish to grow and to estimate the amount you'll need. Keep this list handy when you read the guide to common vegetables, their average yield, and how much space they require (see chapter 6).

HOW MUCH TIME DO YOU HAVE?

You don't want your garden to take up every extra minute of your day, so think carefully about how much time you can dedicate to this project. Are there certain seasons when you go on vacation? Need to take children to soccer practice every weekend? Have a maxed-out schedule because of other obligations? Consider these types of questions.

Be realistic when planning the size of your garden so you don't get overwhelmed. It's better to start small and add to your plantings when time allows. Plan ahead for time spent weeding, watering, pruning, checking for insects, and harvesting. Use time-saving techniques, such as mulching to prevent weeds and installing drip irrigation (system of hoses or pipes that drip water onto the soil next to a specific plant) to reduce watering responsibilities. Locate beds close to the house, if possible, to reduce time spent walking to and from the garden to harvest and maintain your plantings.

METHOD MASH-UPS

If you can't decide which garden methods would work best for your specific needs, don't worry! There's no reason you have to stick with just one. Instead, use a combination of different systems according to your space and growing conditions. For example:

» Install a trellis for climbing crops as a backdrop for a bed that mixes insectary plants with colorful salad vegetables and herbs.

» Turn a large, sunny backyard into a wide-row or biointensive garden with a compost bin and potting shed nearby. Use the sheet mulching technique (see page 11) around sprawling pumpkins and squash.

» Grow vines on an arbor over part of your patio, with vertical stacking containers of strawberries and herbs and large pots for miniature blueberries in sunny areas.

» Use square-foot spacing techniques (see page 13) in an in-ground garden rather than a raised bed.

Of course, these ideas are just a sampling for putting your outdoor space to work for you. Pay careful attention to each area of your yard and look for microclimates that have more sun, while avoiding areas that are windy or more susceptible to frost, and choose the best gardening technique for each spot.

CHAPTER 3

SOIL, GLORIOUS SOIL

Healthy, productive gardens start with soil that's rich in organic matter and teeming with life. Most plants (and the beneficial microbes that boost the plants' nutrient uptake) do best in soil with a pH range from slightly acidic to neutral. Although some crops, such as blueberries, prefer a more acidic soil pH, others, such as asparagus, prefer a more alkaline soil. You may need to loosen compacted soils, add amendments to improve water retention in sandy beds, or make heavy clay more friable.

Adding organic matter in the form of compost and mulch is one of the best investments you can make to improve the productivity and health of your vegetables, herbs, and fruits. Get your garden off to the best start by improving the soil, and you'll harvest greater yields of nutritious food.

THE COMPOSITION OF SOIL

Soil is a pretty amazing substance made up of sand, silt, clay, organic matter (humus), pockets of air and moisture, and a myriad of insects, fungi, and microbes. To the untrained eye it might seem that soil is just "dirt," handy for retaining water and a good place for roots to grow. However, the organic gardener would be wise to view this component of their garden as the foundation for a successful harvest.

Many gardeners grow frustrated working with less-than-ideal soil. Heavy clay has tiny, plate-like particles that are easily compacted and prone to water-logging. The relatively large particles in sandy soils allow water to drain quickly, leaving plants susceptible to drought. Between these extremes are silty soils with medium-size particles. The best soil makeup for gardening is composed of a balance of these basic soil types and is referred to as loam. Loamy soils have the ideal space between particles for the air and moisture necessary for healthy root systems.

SAND   SILT   CLAY   LOAM

In addition to having a balanced structure, truly healthy soil is home to count-less organisms that convert humus and minerals into nutrients needed for plant growth. Many of these beneficial microbes form symbiotic relationships with plant roots, making it possible for nitrogen, phosphorous, potassium, and a host of micronutrients to be absorbed and put to good use by vegetables, herbs, and fruits.

When synthetic pesticides are applied to crops, this web of life is disrupted. I've compared the soil of a conventional agricultural field with the soil in my organic garden and the difference is undeniable. Soil with pesticide residue is nearly devoid of life, but my garden soil is home to a thriving ecosystem of helpful creatures. Without these beneficial organisms, plants require increasing applications of fertilizer to produce a harvest.

Not only is it less expensive to care for your plants by improving your soil structure and encouraging beneficial organisms, it's also much better for the environment and our bodies alike.

Testing Your Soil

Get your garden off to a good start by testing your soil pH, water drainage, and potential lead contamination. These tests will help you avoid problems and increase your harvests.

You may order a pH or lead contamination test kit online or have your soil tested at the local extension office. Collect a sample by removing the sod and taking soil from several spots in your garden bed. Mix what you've gathered and fill the container for testing. If there is lead contamination (a common problem next to old homes, industrial sites, and roadways), don't raise food in the existing soil. Instead, plant vegetables and herbs in containers or in a raised bed with a base to prevent plants from absorbing this dangerous metal. The majority of plants grow well with a soil pH between 5.5 and 7.0, and the pH may be adjusted according to the test kit directions.

If your only option for a garden space is a paved area, you may build raised beds there, as long as water can drain away. Fill the raised bed with soil or potting mix, or use sheet mulching or a lasagna garden to create new soil. The mulch will take longer to decompose because it isn't in direct contact with the soil.

SOIL PREPARATION AND AERATION

Well-aerated soil has plenty of air pockets for holding the moisture and gases needed by roots and beneficial microbes. Soil that is compacted or heavy in clay doesn't have enough air pockets and doesn't drain well, potentially causing root rot and poor overall growth.

To determine if your soil needs aeration to improve drainage, dig a hole 1 foot deep. Fill it with water and allow to drain overnight, then fill again. Press a yardstick into the bottom of the hole and check every hour for the drainage rate; the ideal range is 1 to 3 inches per hour. If water drains too quickly, add lots of compost to retain moisture. If it drains too slowly, aerate the soil by double digging and amending with plenty of compost, or consider planting perennials in a permaculture garden to slowly improve soil structure over time.

AMENDING THE SOIL

Adding organic matter to the soil each year boosts fertility and increases the number of beneficial microbes that, in turn, feed our plants. Soil amendments may be purchased from garden centers or created for free by composting leaves, wood chips, manure, grass clippings, and kitchen waste. We'll learn more about the alchemy of composting "garbage" into rich, black soil in the "Composting" section of this chapter (see pages 30 to 31).

To keep your garden truly organic, make sure the materials used to amend your garden are free of herbicides or other toxic chemicals. Livestock manure is great for soil fertility, but make sure the animals were not treated with medications that could kill microbes or be absorbed by your veggies.

By working organic amendments into your garden over time, you can improve poor soil structure, adjust the pH, and repopulate beneficial organisms even after years of herbicide and pesticide applications have left you with barren soil.

DOUBLE DIGGING

Quickly loosen and aerate your garden soil by double digging your beds. To do so, dig up and remove 8 to 12 inches of topsoil and set on a tarp or some cardboard off to the side. Next, dig up and remove another layer of soil about 8 to 12 inches deep and set aside, separate from the topsoil. Place the topsoil in the bottom of the bed, with the sod-side down. Combine the rest of the soil with plenty of compost and shovel this mixture back into the bed.

This technique is a great way to loosen compacted or clay soil. Double-digging your garden beds allows you to plant quickly, improves drainage, and introduces organic matter for healthy plant roots. If your soil is very sandy, tilling in compost or starting a lasagna garden will improve water retention.

PLANTING DIVERSELY

Perennials, shrubs, and trees absorb minerals from deep beneath our topsoil. As these plants shed organic matter in the form of decaying roots, leaves, and twigs, they provide nutrients to fuel the growth of shallow-rooted crops, including many of our vegetables and herbs. Take advantage of this natural cycle by planting a diversity of perennial crops, then compost plant debris into homemade fertilizer.

Improve the soil in annual beds by rotating crops (see page 50) and including legumes to fix nitrogen in the soil. Work composted leaves into the soil each year to add organic matter, unless the leaves came from plants that were diseased.

TILLING

Tilling can help prepare your garden; however, there are downsides to this technique. Although the top layer of soil is turned and the sod is shredded, grass and weed roots may grow back, making maintenance difficult. In clay soils, the tines of a rototiller also create a compacted zone below the tilled layer.

Overworking sandy soils can cause nutrients to leach away. Instead, add plenty of compost and reduce tilling. Because wet clay soils are easily compacted into dense layers with few air pockets necessary for root health, always allow them to dry out before tilling and do so sparingly.

Making Sustainable Choices

Keep your garden environmentally friendly by choosing sustainable soil amendments. Most potting mixes are composed of peat moss, vermiculite, and perlite (heat-treated volcanic glass that is lightweight and absorbent). Peat bogs are endangered ecosystems that are destroyed when harvested so a more sustainable choice would be compost or coconut coir. Vermiculite and perlite are both mined and heat-treated in an energy-intensive process, so consider replacing these products with horticultural sand, composted sawdust, or finely ground bark mulch.

The best way to ensure that soil amendments and potting mixes are sustainable is to make your own. Compost your own yard waste, kitchen scraps, and other organic matter, or choose eco-friendly amendments such as organic compost, kelp meal, composted manure, or coconut coir (rinse well to remove natural salts).

SOIL ENRICHMENT

Gardeners can provide many of the nutrients needed by vegetables and fruits just by adding sufficient quantities of organic matter to their soil to feed the beneficial microorganisms that feed our plants. However, sometimes there just aren't enough nutrients in the soil and you'll need to supplement with organic fertilizers.

Many fertilizers contain only the macronutrients needed by plants: nitrogen (N), phosphorus (P), and potassium (K). The label lists them as N-P-K and includes the percentage of each respective nutrient. Some organic fertilizers also have trace amounts of micronutrients. Consider using these fertilizers sparingly and only when needed. Applying too much fertilizer leads to sparse root systems that leave plants susceptible to drought and disease.

NATURAL FERTILIZERS

Choose organic fertilizers with low percentages of the macronutrients (5 percent to 15 percent) to make burning the roots and disturbing microbes less likely. Keep in mind that:

- » nitrogen fuels green leafy growth,
- » phosphorous spurs root development, and
- » potassium supports flowering and fruiting.

Before you fertilize any plant, determine its nutrient requirements. For example, salad greens are leafy plants and need more nitrogen, seedlings and new transplants benefit from phosphorous to stimulate rooting, and tomatoes are fruiting plants and won't produce a crop without potassium.

Organic fertilizers are available online and in most garden centers. Common ingredients include bat guano, bone meal, blood meal, fish emulsion, kelp meal, mushroom compost, organic compost, and worm castings.

Those who practice a vegan lifestyle may wish to avoid fertilizers with animal byproducts, such as bone meal. Although these ingredients may be renewable, they aren't humanely produced. Rock phosphate (phosphorous) and greensand (potassium) are both mined from nonrenewable sources. The good news is that many nutrients are commonly present in soil but must first be converted into usable forms for plants by beneficial microbes. So, the cheapest and most sustainable source of fertilizer for our plants may often be coaxed from existing soil just by feeding the microbes with compost.

SOIL-BUILDING PLANTS

One of the most important groups of plants for building fertile soil is legumes, which includes alfalfa, beans, clover, peanuts, peas, and vetch. Their value lies in the ability to "fix" atmospheric nitrogen in the soil into a form that plants can absorb and utilize. If you examine the root system of a legume, you'll find small nodules filled with beneficial bacteria called rhizobia, which convert nitrogen into usable ammonia and, in turn, receive sugars from plant roots.

Another way to build soil with plant materials is to raise cover crops and green manures, such as rye, oats, wheat, or those lovely legumes we've already discussed. These materials are planted in empty beds to reduce erosion, prevent weeds, and fertilize the soil when they are tilled under and composted back into the soil.

SOIL MIXES AND POTTING MEDIUM

Raising vegetables and other crops in containers and raised beds requires a suitable potting medium or soil mix to fill them. Most potting mediums contain no soil at all and are instead formulated with peat moss, perlite, vermiculite, and maybe some compost. A few companies are switching from peat-based formulas to more sustainable choices, such as coconut coir, so check the label before you buy.

You can save money and increase sustainability by starting a lasagna garden to build your own soil, or filling beds with homemade potting mix. To make your own mix, combine equal parts coconut coir, compost, and composted wood chips and leaves for a general mix, or replace the composted wood chips with horticultural sand for root crops. In a pinch, you can use plain compost mixed with a little sand.

If you decide to purchase a ready-to-use potting mix, keep in mind that it may contain synthetic fertilizers to feed plants. Another common additive in potting mixes are water retention crystals that absorb and hold excess moisture until plants need it. This combination sounds like a great way to keep plants hydrated; however, these crystals may contain cancer-causing compounds (primarily a problem when inhaled) and are best avoided in an organic garden.

Another option is to combine topsoil with compost to fill your containers and raised beds, but keep in mind that purchased topsoil may come from herbicide-treated farmland. In the past, I have purchased topsoil containing so much herbicide residue that seeds would not germinate, and seedlings transplanted into this soil died soon after. Saving a little money on a bag of topsoil ended up setting back my garden bed by a full growing season.

Soil and the Raised Bed

Determine how much potting mix or soil you'll need to fill a raised bed by measuring its length, width, and depth (in linear feet) and plugging those numbers into the following equation:

length x width x depth = cubic feet of soil or potting mix needed

For example, with a raised bed 4 feet by 6 feet by ½ foot deep, you'll get 4 x 6 x .5 = 12. So you'd need a total of 12 cubic feet of soil to fill this raised bed.

Keep in mind that 1 inch is about 0.08333 foot. For a bed that's 4 feet by 6 feet by 8 inches, you'd need to multiply 8 inches by 0.08333 to find the depth in feet, like this:

8 x 0.08333 = 0.66664 feet

Round up to two decimal points (0.67 feet) to plug into the equation:

4 x 6 x 0.67 = 16.08 cubic feet

If you have trouble determining how much soil you'll need, check out the Gardener's Supply website for a handy calculator app (see Resources, page 118).

COMPOSTING

Composting is the process of converting organic waste into humus with the help of beneficial soil organisms and is a great way to reduce household waste and create nutrient-rich soil for your garden. Although many waste materials can be composted, some contain pathogens or attract vermin. Never include feces from predators (such as cats and dogs) in compost because of the danger of parasites. Dairy products, fatty or oily materials, and meats attract rodents and should also be avoided. Citrus peels contain a compound that kills insects, so don't add many. If you compost manure from livestock, make sure the animals weren't treated with worming medications or antibiotics.

For the best results, use the following ratio: 2 parts brown matter (wood chips, straw, and leaves, for example) to 1 part green matter (including fresh grass clippings, kitchen waste, and weeds), and layer with garden soil to introduce beneficial bacteria to the mix.

COLD COMPOSTING

Cold composting generally takes at least six months. Layer 2 parts brown matter with 1 part green matter, and top with soil. Water the materials and add new layers as you have organic waste available. Because cold compost piles are allowed to break down slowly, the heat created during decomposition is minimal and will not kill weed seeds and pathogens.

HOT COMPOSTING

Hot composting can take as little as 1 month. The pile is turned often, accelerating decomposition and encouraging the growth of bacteria, which, in turn, increases the amount of heat released during decomposition to kill weed seeds and disease spores.

To get started, build a pile at least 3 feet by 3 feet. Layer 2 parts brown matter to 1 part green matter and top with garden soil. Continue building layers until the pile is at least 2 to 3 feet tall. Lightly water and use a compost thermometer to check the internal temperature every 2 to 3 days. When the temperature reaches 110°F to 140°F, turn the pile and add more water, if needed. The materials should feel damp but not soggy. When your compost is brown and smells like soil, it's ready to use.

Troubleshooting Your Compost Pile

If the compost is too wet and has a bad odor
Add only enough water to keep compost damp. If a handful of compost feels wet, add more brown matter and turn the pile to reduce odor and absorb excess water.

If the compost stinks but isn't overly wet
Adding too many acidic or high-nitrogen materials (especially grass clippings, coffee grounds, and other kinds of kitchen waste) creates low-oxygen conditions that lead to the growth of anaerobic bacteria and a stinky pile. Work in more brown materials, such as straw or dry leaves, and turn the pile to counteract the high nitrogen content.

If the compost doesn't break down quickly or get hot
The pile may be too dry, there may be too much brown matter, or beneficial organisms may be lacking in your soil. Reach into the center of the pile to see if it feels damp. Water the pile if it feels dry. If moisture levels aren't the problem, try adding more green material or add a compost activator (product containing beneficial bacteria) to the pile and turn it to incorporate these additions.

If rodents are attracted to the compost
Don't add meat, fat, or dairy products to your pile. Rodents also enjoy vegetable peelings, eggshells, and other kitchen scraps, so you may need to work these items into the very center of the pile to deter mice, or try a worm-composting system in an area where rodents can't reach it.

If the compost gets too hot
In some cases, a compost pile can produce so much heat that beneficial microbes in the center die. Make your compost pile smaller, turn the pile more often, or add more coarse materials to create pockets of air in the layers that will help reduce the temperature.

CHAPTER 4

PLANNING, PLANTING, AND TENDING YOUR GARDEN

Now that you have a lovely spot for your garden with healthy soil and plenty of sunlight, you're probably anxious to dig in and start planting. There are so many possibilities for delicious fruits, nutritious vegetables, and aromatic herbs to raise for your table that you might feel a bit overwhelmed by the choices. With a bit of thought and planning, you can eliminate the crops that won't do well in your growing conditions and focus on planting the best foods for your space that also suit your tastes.

Once you've decided on what to grow, you'll need to know how to read a seed packet, successfully sow your seeds, and decide whether to start or buy your seedlings. Maintaining your garden includes controlling weeds, irrigating crops, and knowing when to harvest the bounty. Tidying up your garden is also an important step to reduce disease and prepare the soil for another crop. Let's find out more!

DECIDING WHAT TO GROW

As you look through seed catalogs, you might get confused by the many crops, varieties, and descriptions listed. To keep things simple, consider planting the crops best suited to your climate, growing conditions, and space, as well as those that are most expensive to purchase or are the most productive and nutritious for your investment. Above all, be sure to choose the foods you enjoy eating most! Make a list of all the veggies, herbs, and fruits you enjoy, then narrow your list down as you read this section.

MATCH PLANTS TO YOUR CLIMATE

Choose the best crops for your area to reduce disease and pests caused by stress. Check the USDA Plant Hardiness Map (see page 114) to find your growing region and the Old Farmer's Alamanac website in the Resources section (see page 118) to find the average date of your last frost in spring and first frost in fall; these dates will guide the process. When choosing plants, it's also important to know if they are annuals, biennials, or perennials:

Annuals produce a harvest and seeds in their first year.

Biennials produce vegetative growth the first season, then flower and produce seed the second year. In general, these crops are harvested in the first year (e.g., beets and carrots).

Perennials take several years to produce, but they continue to grow and fruit for many years.

Here are some handy tips for choosing your crops and planting times:

» Choose perennials the USDA Plant Hardiness Map indicates are hardy in your area.

» Cool season crops grow best between 40°F and 75°F and bolt (go to seed) in higher temperatures. Warm season crops do not tolerate frost and grow best at 75°F or warmer.

» Start seeds indoors (see page 36) or in a cold frame (unheated enclosure with a transparent lid that protects from cold while allowing sunlight) to extend your growing season.

» Make sure crops are planted early enough so they can mature before your first frost.

MATCH PLANTS TO YOUR SITE

Keep sunlight requirements in mind when planning your garden. Some plants like full, hot sun all day whereas others need shade to prevent bolting or wilting in hot weather.

» A plant that needs full sun should have bright, direct light for 6+ hours per day.

» A plant that needs part shade will do best with bright, direct light in the morning and evening with shade during the hot part of the day.

Additionally, some plants like a moist, rich soil, whereas others need a loose, sandy bed. Allow enough space for each crop to reach their mature size when planting or thinning. The guide starting on page 73 will help you pick a spot well suited to each vegetable, herb, or fruit you wish to grow.

CONSIDER THE RETURN ON YOUR PLANTING INVESTMENT

When time or space is at a premium it is especially important to choose the most productive crops for your investment. Of course, you'll want to plant the foods you enjoy eating, but also consider how much you can expect to harvest and which store-bought crops come with the most packaging or pesticide residue. For example, if you love fresh salads, you've probably noticed how much plastic is used to package lettuce and spinach. You can grow a lot of healthy greens in a small space, saving money and reducing household waste.

AVOID MONOCULTURES

To reduce pests and disease, plant a diversity of crops rather than large blocks of all one species or plant family. Some members of the same plant family are susceptible to the same insects or fungal infections, which is why keeping these crops separated helps slow the spread.

Interplanting vegetables, herbs, and fruits with a variety of flowers and other plants that attract beneficial insects and birds is key to managing an organic garden naturally. In chapter 6, you'll find plant profiles, including the family each crop belongs to, so you can avoid interplanting species that share pests and diseases.

THINK THROUGH TO HARVEST

As you're planning, think about the foods you enjoy eating fresh and those you purchase frozen, canned, dried, or pickled. Will you have the time and know-how to put up some of your harvest for later? The easiest way to preserve your harvests is by freezing or dehydrating, but you can also make fresh-pack pickles without much fuss. Canning is a bit more involved, but this method creates shelf-stable food and is well worth the effort.

GETTING STARTED

Check your list of plants to determine which should be started indoors (see "Starting Seeds Indoors" below), sown directly into your garden (see "Direct Sowing" on page 37), and purchased as seedlings. There are pros and cons to each method.

The benefits of starting your own seedlings include:

» The cost of a seed packet is often the same as one started plant.

» There are more varieties to choose from, including heirlooms.

» You control the pesticides and fertilizers applied to seedlings.

» You can increase sustainability with recycled pots and homemade potting mix.

» You may start only as many plants as you need.

The benefits of purchasing seedlings include:

» Your purchase may support a local greenhouse.

» You won't need to buy special lights for starting seeds.

» The process takes less time.

» No special care is needed until you purchase your plants.

STARTING SEEDS INDOORS

Raising your own seedlings can be as simple as sowing a few seeds in trays in a window or as complex as setting up a seed-starting system. For the least expensive option, start seeds on a sunny windowsill just a few weeks before moving the seedlings outdoors.

For the strongest transplants, set up a full-spectrum LED grow light above your seedlings. A shelving unit fitted with light fixtures can house many seed trays. Seedling heat mats provide gentle bottom heat for speeding up germination, but you can set seeds anywhere with a temperature of 65°F to 80°F. Cover trays with a sheet of clear plastic or another transparent lid to hold in moisture until the seeds germinate. Spritz

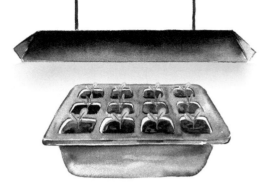

the seedlings with a spray bottle of water only when the surface of the potting mix dries out, and use a small fan to mimic wind, encourage strong stems, and reduce "damping off," a fungal disease.

Purchase seed-starting trays made from recycled plastic, reuse plastic yogurt containers, or make newspaper pots to increase sustainability. You'll need a soilless seed-starting mix, or you can make your own from compost.

When outdoor temperatures are warm enough for your seedlings, you'll need to harden them off, meaning move them outdoors for a bit more time each day until they have acclimated to their new surroundings. Start by placing them out of direct light for a few minutes and increasing exposure to sun and wind each day. Pay close attention to prevent sunburn, drying out, or freezing, and don't plant them in the garden until the nighttime temperatures are warm enough for each crop.

DIRECT SOWING

Some crops grow best when sown directly into their garden bed. Read the directions on your seed packets for the best time to sow, how deep to plant seeds, how far apart to space them, and how much space to leave between seedlings after thinning (removing extra seedlings to provide the proper space between mature plants).

Some cool-season crops may be planted as early as the soil can be worked in the spring until several weeks before the last frost, whereas heat-loving crops should be sown once all danger of frost has passed. Check the average date of the last frost in your area to determine when to plant each crop.

Keep seedbeds moist by watering them gently each day. Even moisture is critical during germination and drying out could ruin your entire planting. Some seeds take two or three weeks to germinate, so be prepared to water them twice a day.

My Organic Garden Worksheet

WHAT METHODS DO I WANT TO TRY?

Consider the pros and cons of each gardening methods you wish to try, thinking about where each could fit into the space you have available.

☐ Biointensive

☐ Container

☐ Edible Landscape

☐ Lasagna

☐ Raised-Bed

☐ Sheet Mulch

☐ Single-Row

☐ Square-Foot

☐ Straw-Bale

☐ Vertical

☐ Wide-Row

HOW MUCH SPACE DO I HAVE?

Sketch your garden, raised beds, or containers and their measurements to gain an understanding of your available space. Note the amount of sun each area receives to help choose the best crops for each spot.

HOW MUCH TIME DO I HAVE?

Be realistic about your time commitment and don't plant more than you can care for. It's better to start with humble expectations and add to your garden later than to overestimate what you can maintain. Try blocking out time for your garden on a calendar to help you plan.

☐ Daily:

☐ Weekly:

☐ Monthly:

WHAT CROPS WILL I GROW?

List the vegetables, herbs, fruits, and beneficial plants you wish to raise.

VEGETABLES	HERBS	FRUITS	BENEFICIAL PLANTS

CROP CLOSE-UP

For each vegetable, herb, or fruit you wish to grow, list the best time of year to plant and whether you will start seeds indoors (see page 36), direct sow (see page 37), or purchase seedlings from a garden center. Consider how much you can use fresh or if you'll have time to preserve the extras.

CROP	PLANTING DATES	SOWING METHOD	

	TIME TO HARVEST	HOW MUCH TO PLANT	HOW TO USE (FRESH OR PRESERVED)

How to Read a Seed Packet

Most seed companies include a wealth of information on their seed packets, including whether the seeds were raised organically (these seeds aren't treated with fungicides); if the variety of seed is an heirloom, hybrid, or an All-American Selection (or AAS, which are chosen for superior performance); and if the variety is resistant to any diseases.

There is some confusion about seeds that are hybrids versus GMOs (genetically modified organisms, with genetic material inserted in a lab setting into the plant's DNA). Hybrid seeds are not the same as a GMO and are created by cross-pollinating two or more varieties of the same species. An F1 hybrid is created by crossing two open-pollinated varieties (which breed true to type), and an F2 hybrid is created by crossing an F1 hybrid with an open-pollinated variety.

Other important information to look for on your seed packet is the best time to plant, time to maturity (or days to harvest), time to germination (how long it takes seeds to sprout), how much sun the plant needs, how far apart to plant the seeds, and how far apart the plants should be after thinning. For the best results, follow these instructions closely.

SEEDS
SPINACH
250 seeds

Sell by/Packed for 2021

Spinach (Bloomsdale Long Standing)
Spinacea oleracea

Culture:

Harvest:

| Soil Temp. 45–75°F | Sowing Depth ½" | Final Plant Spacing 4–6" |
| Final Row Spacing 8–12" | Light Full Sun | Days to Maturity 37–42 |

GETTING ENOUGH WATER

Keeping your garden properly irrigated is especially important when plants don't have an extensive root system, such as when they are seedlings. You'll need to check the soil moisture regularly in hot, dry weather and provide irrigation when needed.

On the other hand, if your soil is high in clay and the drainage is poor, make sure plants aren't overwatered. Too much water is just as unhealthy as too little and can cause roots to rot and lose their ability to absorb moisture and nutrients. The symptom of root rot is wilted leaves, the same as too little water. Always check the soil and water only when needed.

CONTOURING

This watering method has been used in rice paddies for centuries to hold water or direct its flow to a planting bed. Permaculture proponents use this technique in much the same way to reduce irrigation needs. To put contouring to work in your own garden, you'll need to study the lay of your land to see how water runs off and where it tends to collect. Situate beds or rows of plants to slow water runoff and reduce soil erosion. For example, rows are planted across, rather than up and down, a slope that slows the flow of water and increases the absorption of moisture into the soil.

IRRIGATION METHODS

Most gardeners need to water crops during periods of low rainfall, so it's a good idea to plan ahead for irrigation. Watering a garden with a sprinkler wastes a lot of water and can cause fungal diseases. If you must use a sprinkler, do so in the morning so leaves dry off before nightfall. Some better irrigation options are outlined here:

» Use soaker hoses to water at the root zone and reduce evaporation.

» Fill milk jugs with water, replace the cap, and poke a tiny hole in the bottom to water individual plants.

» Direct water to individual plants with drip irrigation.

» Hand-water with a hose or watering can to allow close inspection of plants as you work.

Save even more water by installing rain barrels on your downspouts, if rainwater harvesting is allowed in your area. Mulching and planting in slightly sunken beds reduces evaporation, and amending soil with compost helps the soil retain water. If your area is prone to dry spells, choose plants that are drought tolerant when possible. Try using a blend of water-saving techniques to reduce irrigation needs.

GETTING DOWN IN THE WEEDS

Gardeners spend a great deal of time waging war against weeds, which is understandable considering they grow like crazy and compete with our vegetables for water and nutrients. However, there are ways to keep these unwanted plants under control without spending your entire summer weeding, cultivating, and spraying with toxic chemicals.

Keep weeds to a minimum by removing them before they spread seeds in your garden beds. You can also plant your crops densely to reduce competition and use mulch to prevent weed seeds from germinating. With this combination, you'll find it much easier to keep your garden relatively free from unwanted plants.

MULCHING

Significantly reduce your weeding duties and reduce moisture loss with layers of mulch between rows and plants. Create your own compost to mulch small plants and consider using a chipper or shredder to create mulch from your own yard waste.

Keep weeds down between beds or rows by covering these bare areas with clean straw, free cardboard, or wood chips. Make sure any bales of straw brought into your garden are free of thistle seed and that the straw wasn't sprayed with persistent herbicides. Wood chips may be available for free from landscaping companies, offering an affordable and sustainable option. Keep in mind that as wood chips break down they tie up nitrogen in the soil, so you may need to use more fertilizer.

Reduce weeds in planting beds by mulching with compost, straw, shredded leaves, or another mulch with a fine texture. To prevent fungal problems, don't pile mulch over seedlings or newly seeded beds or against the stems of plants. It's better to add an inch or two of mulch at a time around plants instead of adding thick layers all at once.

DENSITY PLANTINGS

Spacing your plants closely helps them by shading sprouting weeds that rob them of moisture and nutrients. Be careful not to plant your crops too closely, which reduces air circulation and encourages the spread of disease. Another option is to plant shorter crops that like a shady spot where they can keep weeds at bay without interfering with taller crops.

Interplanting two or more vegetables or herbs together can be helpful to both crops. Some good combinations are tomatoes surrounded by spinach. Spinach is a low-growing crop that may be seeded densely, shading out weeds without competing with the tomatoes. As your tomato plants fill in, they will shade the ground around the time your spinach crop is harvested.

Pinching, Pruning, or Staking

Many plants are more productive when their growth is directed by selectively pinching, pruning, or staking. For example, tomatoes produce side shoots that take energy away from flowering and fruiting on the main stem. By pinching off these suckers, you'll increase the number of ripe tomatoes harvested. Pruning the inner branches of fruit trees allows more sunlight to reach the fruit, increasing sugar content. Staking vines keeps fruit off the ground and prevents rot.

PRUNING

Pinch flower buds and side shoots easily when growth is tender to increase the vigor of the plant. For example, basil will produce more leaves when flower buds are removed. Pruning mature growth also keeps plants from taking over an area and directs energy to the best branches; however, this technique requires pruners or a pruning saw. Grape vines, fruit trees, and other woody plants require annual pruning.

PINCHING

Try growing microgreens or sprouts in your garden or indoors over winter. These nutritious greens are clipped for salads or stir-fries. Once they are clipped, they usually won't regrow, so plant frequently for a continual harvest.

Staking plants may be as simple as using a tomato cage or bamboo stakes. Wire fencing will support a row of peas or pole beans, but grapes need a heavy-duty trellis or fence to support their vines.

STAKING

HARVEST

A well-planned bed may produce vegetables, fruits, and herbs throughout the season. Be sure to harvest these goodies as they ripen, because some plants will shut down future production if you don't keep them picked. Plus, you don't want your veggies to end up tough or overripe.

Check plants daily for any vegetables or fruits that are ready to use. The best time of day to harvest is after the dew dries in the morning (to prevent spreading fungal spores on wet leaves) and before the heat of the day (when some veggies may wilt). Harvest tomatoes and melons before watering to prevent cracking. Pick string beans every two or three days. Use a knife to cut squash and eggplants from the plant. Here are a few tools and supplies that make harvest easier:

» Basket or bowl to hold the harvest

» Kitchen shears or a knife for cutting tough stems

» Gloves to protect your hands from thorny plants

» Jar of water for keeping herbs or flowers fresh

GARDEN CLEANUP

Removing spent plants from your garden helps reduce pests and disease. At the end of the season after a fall frost, a cleanup is required. A cleanup is also required when a crop is finished. Compost all organic matter (unless it's diseased), and prepare the bed for your next planting.

With a bit of care and planning, you may be able to plant several successive crops in one row or bed. Sow seeds every week or two for an extended harvest, or follow up a cool-season crop with warm-season vegetables. Remove spent plants, add compost, and plant another crop to make good use of your space. If you'll be replacing one crop with a related planting (plants from the same family, such as legumes), cleaning up the first crop is especially important. Better yet, follow up with an unrelated crop. In this scenario, each growing season you could potentially plant three successive crops in one space. One of my favorite succession plantings is a crop of early beets, followed by string beans, with a final sowing of kale in the fall.

For gardeners in frost-free zones or areas with only a light freeze, be sure to do a thorough cleanup and practice plant rotation to prevent the buildup of pathogens in the soil.

THE NEXT TIME AROUND: CROP ROTATION

Rotating crops might sound complicated, but it's easy if you keep track of your garden layout each year. To reduce problems with disease, pests, and nutrient deficiencies, raise different crops (from different plant families) in each garden bed following this schedule:

- » **Year 1:** legumes to build soil fertility (alfalfa, beans, peas)
- » **Year 2:** heavy feeders (greens, pumpkins, sweet corn)
- » **Year 3:** medium feeders (flowers, peppers, tomatoes)
- » **Year 4:** root crops (beets, carrots, potatoes)

Although this plan is ideal, many gardeners plant only one type of vegetable or they have a small space, making it difficult to rotate their crops. Fortunately, there are some ways to overcome these issues.

To "rotate" a container garden, you may either switch the crop grown in each pot or sanitize the pot and refill it with fresh potting mix each year. Sanitizing and putting in fresh soil may also be used in small raised beds; however, the cost of refilling beds with fresh soil can be considerable. Try marking off the bed using the square-foot method (see page 13) and keep meticulous track of which crops are grown in each space to help plan your rotation schedule. Another option is to plant a straw-bale garden (see page 13) and add the straw to your hot compost pile at the end of the season to kill most pathogens.

CHAPTER 5

NATURAL PEST AND DISEASE MANAGEMENT

The organic gardener who adds compost to their soil, avoids toxins, and uses natural methods of pest and disease prevention will enjoy a healthier garden than those who reach for synthetic fertilizers and pesticides. However, even the most vigorous plants are sure to have occasional issues with pests and disease. Before you reach for a quick fix, take time to identify the problem and learn how to deal with it as naturally and safely as possible. Try the least toxic solution to avoid killing the beneficial insects and microbes so important to plant health.

Keep your vegetables, fruits, and herbs free from stress to help prevent serious damage. When a problem does arise, it will be easier to treat if your garden is a healthy ecosystem instead of a monoculture dependent on synthetic chemicals.

THE BEST DEFENSE IS A HAPPY PLANT

Every plant needs sunlight, water, and nutrients to support photosynthesis, the process by which they create simple sugars to fuel their growth. If any of these basic needs are not met, plants become stressed and release chemicals that attract pests to an all-you-can-eat buffet.

We've already discussed the importance of feeding beneficial soil life with compost to encourage healthy root systems and uptake of available nutrients. Keep in mind that applying too many fertilizers or pesticides (even some natural ones) reduces root growth and destroys helpful insects and microbes, leaving your plants more susceptible to drought, pests, and disease.

Your garden must also have enough water to support plant growth without waterlogging the soil or leaching nutrients. Water only when needed and keep leaves dry to prevent fungal diseases. For the same reason, space plants properly to allow air circulation around leaves.

Keep your garden healthy and plant a wide variety of crops and landscape plants and you'll have fewer issues with pests and disease.

BUILDING YOUR GARDEN'S NATURAL DEFENSES

As your second line of defense against pests and disease, provide habitat to attract your natural allies: the insects, arachnids, birds, toads, and bats that pollinate crops and patrol your garden, happily gobbling up pests. Include sources of food, water, and shelter, as well as places to rear their young and, in time, you could have an army of beneficial creatures in residence.

PREDATORY AND PARASITIC INSECTS

Sometimes it seems that bugs are intent on destroying our gardens. However, there are plenty of beneficial insects and arachnids that consume those annoying garden pests. Predatory insects and spiders consume aphids, grubs, slugs, and thrips. Parasitic species lay their eggs on a host to provide for their young. If you see a caterpillar with small white egg sacs on its back, leave it alone so the parasitic wasp eggs may hatch and patrol your garden in the future.

Here are some helpful insects and arachnids and the "bad guys" they control:

GOOD GUYS	BAD GUYS
assassin bug	beetles, caterpillars, flies, mosquitoes
big-eyed bug	aphids, caterpillars, insect eggs, leafhoppers, whiteflies
green lacewing	aphids, leafhopper nymphs, mealybugs, moth eggs, scale, spider mites, thrips, whiteflies
ground beetles	aphids, armyworms, cutworms, maggots, slugs, wireworms
hoverfly/syrphid fly larvae	aphids, caterpillars, mealybugs
lady beetle	aphids, beetle and moth eggs, mites, thrips
parasitic wasps	aphids, beetles, caterpillars, flies, scale
praying mantis	aphids, beetles, caterpillars, crickets, grass-hoppers, mosquitoes
spiders	aphids, flies, leafhoppers, june bugs, moths
yellowjackets	aphids, cabbage worms and other caterpillars, fly larvae

Attract these insects and spiders to your landscape by planting a variety of nectar-producing plants, providing water sources, and including habitat where they may lay eggs, overwinter, and seek shelter from their own predators.

Shallow pans of water or mud puddles are great sources of drinking water for birds and other helpful wildlife. Small insects usually get the moisture they need from dew or from the juicy insects and eggs they consume. Butterflies, bees, and larger insects benefit from a dish of wet sand where they can land and get a drink. Place pieces of cut fruit—such as apples, bananas, and oranges—in your garden to provide insects with an "energy drink" that is helpful when they are migrating or when there are few food sources nearby.

INSECTARY PLANTS

Insectary plants provide habitat and a food source, such as pollen and nectar, for beneficial insects and arachnids that offer biological pest control in your garden. Include a wide variety of plants with small compound flowers (having many small flowerlets such as cilantro, dill, and yarrow) that attract predatory and parasitic insects. Including some of these plants in your garden is a great way to encourage adult insects to come for the free food and stay to lay their eggs. Some species provide pest control during their larval stage, so be sure to attract the adults to lay their eggs near the pests you'd like to control, such as an infestation of aphids.

If beneficial insects visit your yard but don't find a food source, water, shelter, or places to lay eggs, they will move on to look for a more suitable ecosystem. Encourage them to stay by planting a border of wildflowers, herbs, and native plants. Provide a source of water and plant native trees and shrubs when possible.

Check out the table of insectary plants (see Appendix, page 107) for common species that provide food for these helpful creatures.

POLLINATOR PLANTS

Flowers that provide food sources for pollinators are an important part of a healthy garden. Pollinator plants increase visits from bees, butterflies, and hummingbirds that flit from flower to flower, drinking nectar and transporting pollen as they go. Some of our most important food crops won't produce a harvest without pollination.

Happily, many insectary plants also attract pollinators, so you can encourage all sorts of beneficial creatures by choosing a variety of species from our pollinator and insectary plant lists (see Appendix, pages 107 and 111). In addition to the small, nectar-rich compound flowers in the insectary list, include tubular flowers that attract hummingbirds as well as bees and other pollinators. Coral bells, foxglove, and heirloom petunias are great choices.

Keep in mind that hybrid flowers are usually bred to delight the human eye instead of feeding pollinators. Select heirloom and native flower varieties that produce nectar and pollen over showy petals.

Be aware that using systemic insecticides on plants can kill pollinators when they sip the insecticide-laced nectar. Never use these poisons on any plant, even if you don't intend to eat the plant.

Best Planting Practices for Insectary and Pollinator Plants

There is an art to attracting beneficial insects to your home landscape and encouraging them to take up residence. Start by including as many different species of plants for them as possible. Make sure there is a succession of nectar- and pollen-producing plants available throughout the gardening season so they need never leave.

Include several plants from each species so there is enough food in a small space to keep your beneficial creatures well fed. Planting in clusters of three, five, or seven plants also provides structural design, so you'll enjoy these groupings almost as much as the wildlife will. In addition, it's helpful to put some space between species from the same plant family to prevent disease and pest problems.

Beds of pollinator and insectary plants are very pleasing to look at. Try incorporating them into a cottage garden, flower bed, or herb garden, or interplant them in your main garden. Many culinary herbs provide nectar for beneficial insects when they flower, so plant a selection of basil, borage, chives, cilantro, sage, and other herbs. Allow some plants to flower and your insect helpers will find them, too.

TOADS AND OTHER HELPFUL CREATURES

In addition to beneficial insects, a variety of other creatures provide natural pest control in the garden. Bats, birds, frogs, opossums, salamanders, and toads can all put a big dent in pest populations. Although some birds can be a nuisance by digging up newly planted seeds and eating your fruit, many songbirds search all day for caterpillars, flies, and grubs. Bats flit about at night, catching gnats, mosquitoes, and moths. Frogs, salamanders, and toads all feast on flies, larvae, mosquitoes, and slugs. Opossums are notorious for searching out grubs, slugs, and ticks, but keep in mind that they also like to raid compost bins for kitchen scraps.

Provide trees and shrubs in your landscape for birds to perch on and nest in. Birdhouses and bat houses are a great investment for your garden; just be sure to site them properly and clean them yearly. Toad houses and cool, moist spots attract toads and salamanders for a siesta in the heat of the day. Provide a small pond or other source of water for frogs, salamanders, and toads to lay their eggs or they will leave in search of breeding grounds elsewhere.

NATURAL PEST AND DISEASE CONTROL

Even the most robust garden is susceptible to occasional damage from harmful insects, microbes, and fungi. Keep your garden healthy and productive by preventing problems before they occur and checking regularly for symptoms of pests and disease. When an insect or disease becomes a problem, be ready to handpick the pests or treat the plants with a nontoxic solution quickly, before your harvest is affected.

Keep in mind that not all organic or natural means of pest control are safe for beneficial insects, and some can even be detrimental to our own health. Always read the labels of purchased pesticides and be meticulous about following the directions.

HANDPICKING

Handpicking insects off plants is the safest method available to gardeners because it allows you to kill only pests and leave the good guys alone, without any side effects. This method works well for slow-moving insects, such as Colorado potato beetle larvae and cabbage worms. By picking insects off by hand, you can collect a sample in a jar, research the species, and determine whether it's a threat to the health of your plant or actually beneficial.

If you're squeamish about removing the insects, put on a pair of garden gloves and grab a jar of soapy water before you head out for handpicking duties. Flick the pest into the soapy water to drown. For gardeners who also keep poultry, ducks love to eat slugs and guinea fowl consume ticks and other creepy crawlies. Chickens tend to do more damage to veggies than pests, so keep them out of the garden.

PEST CONTROL SPRAYS

INSECTICIDAL SOAPS

Insecticidal soaps are a popular option for organic control of soft-bodied pests, such as aphids, mealybugs, and whiteflies. These sprays kill insects by coating their bodies with a soapy residue that suffocates them. Purchased products are more effective than homemade versions; however, the cost and plastic waste can be a concern for home gardeners. Make your own insecticidal sprays with common household ingredients and test on one or two leaves of affected plants to check for safety. Don't use dish soap with degreasers, disinfectants, fragrances, or moisturizers that may harm plants and beneficial microbes.

Here's a recipe for homemade insecticidal soap:

1 teaspoon plain dish soap
1 quart water

Place ingredients in a clean spray bottle and shake vigorously before spraying plants. Insects must be completely coated for best results.

You may also create your own spray to treat powdery mildew:

1 tablespoon milk
1 teaspoon baking soda
2 or 3 drops plain dish soap

Place ingredients in a clean spray bottle and shake vigorously before spraying plants.

Do not apply insecticidal soaps to plants that are stressed by drought, in full sunlight, or under hot conditions. Do not spray the plants with other pesticides until the soap is washed off, and use this concoction sparingly to prevent a buildup of salts in the soil from the baking soda (sodium bicarbonate).

GARLIC SPRAY

Researchers have found that garlic interplanted with cabbage helps reduce damage from diamondback moths by repelling adults from laying eggs on plants. Although much information about the effectiveness of garlic spray as a pest repellent is anecdotal, this homemade remedy may help prevent damage to brassicas and other crops by repelling aphids, cabbage worms, spider mites, and even rabbits.

Here's how to make your own garlic spray pest repellent:

1 quart (4 cups) water, divided
3 or 4 garlic cloves
1 to 2 teaspoons plain dish soap

Blend 2 cups of water and the garlic in a blender on high. Add the remaining 2 cups of water and the dish soap and mix thoroughly. Strain this mixture through several layers of cheesecloth to remove bits of garlic that could clog your sprayer. Before you spray the entire plant, test this mixture on one or two leaves to make sure the plant is not adversely affected.

The soap in this spray will kill insects by coating their bodies, so avoid spraying beneficial insects and pollinators. The dish soap also acts as a sticking agent to coat leaves with the garlic compounds, increasing the effectiveness of its repellent qualities.

▪ HOT PEPPER SPRAY

Safely repel mammals such as deer, squirrels, and rabbits by planting hot peppers around the edges of your garden or in beds prone to damage. Hot pepper spray offers another option for small spaces with damage from these cute pests. The active ingredient in hot peppers is a compound called capsaicin. This chemical also repels some insects; however, it's unlikely to remove infestations.

Here's a recipe for hot pepper spray:

1 quart water
2 tablespoons crushed red pepper or cayenne pepper flakes
1 teaspoon plain dish soap

Combine the water and crushed red pepper in a saucepan and bring to a boil. Remove the pan from the heat and allow it to sit overnight. Strain the liquid through several layers of cheesecloth to remove solids that might clog your sprayer. Add the dish soap and shake vigorously before spraying.

Test this spray on a few leaves before applying to the entire plant. Always wear a mask and gloves when handling this spray and be careful not to breathe in the fumes or get it in your eyes. To deter more pests, add 2 cloves of crushed garlic to the liquid before heating.

ROW COVERS AND OTHER BARRIERS

Floating row covers (protective lightweight, breathable fabric covers) are a great way to keep flying insects from laying eggs on your cabbage, summer squash, and other vegetables. Protect crops with row covers after the plants have sprouted but before the pests show up in your garden. Make sure the edges of the material are weighted down to keep the cover from blowing in the wind. For crops that require pollination, remove the cover to allow pollinators to do their job, or hand-pollinate the flowers yourself, then reposition the row cover or leave it off. Brussels sprouts and broccoli do not need to be pollinated to provide a harvest, but peppers, pumpkins, and summer squash (to name a few) do.

Waxy coatings on leaves, such as hot pepper wax, also work by creating a barrier that pests can't chew through to reach their meal. Cardboard collars around seedlings prevent cutworms from killing your little plants at their most vulnerable stage. Recycle paper towel tubes or aluminum foil into barriers around your seedlings for this purpose.

TRAPS AND BAITS

These forms of control lure pests to their untimely death with a color, food, or scent they can't resist. Pheromone traps include a natural hormone that attracts specific insects looking for mates. These traps are often used to alert gardeners to the presence of mating insects so they may be controlled with insecticides. Use natural solutions whenever possible. Yellow sticky traps are helpful for reducing whiteflies; you can make your own by coating yellow paper with petroleum jelly. Reduce thrip populations with white sticky traps. Keep in mind that beneficial insects can inadvertently be killed in these traps, too.

Slugs can cause a lot of damage to your garden, especially overnight. You can try a cup of beer sunken with the top at ground level to entice these pests to their demise, or purchase an organic slug bait if the infestation is severe. This product is usually composed of a small dose of iron phosphate mixed into pellet form with tasty wheat gluten or bran that slugs love to eat.

DIATOMACEOUS EARTH

Diotomaceous earth (DE) is a powder made from the shells of tiny marine creatures called diatoms. It works by causing microscopic cuts in soft-bodied insects, slugs, and snails. Always wear a mask when using DE to prevent irritation to your nose, throat, and lungs. Create a natural barrier by sprinkling DE around plants to protect them from cutworms, flea beetle larvae, and slugs. Treat insects on leaves and stems by misting the plant with water then dusting immediately with DE so the powder sticks. This method kills aphids, Colorado potato beetle larvae, and other soft-bodied insects. You'll need to reapply after rain or irrigation washes away the last application.

Keep in mind that DE can also kill beneficial insects, such as bees and lady beetle larvae, by causing lacerations to their bodies. To avoid eliminating garden helpers, do not apply DE to flowers where bees are likely to be affected or to any plants where beneficial insects may be present.

MILKY SPORE DISEASE

When Japanese beetles and their grubs are causing serious damage to your turf or garden, consider using milky spore disease to reduce their populations. This disease is caused by *Paenibacillus popilliae*, a type of bacteria that attacks only Japanese beetle grubs. A powdered form of the bacteria is applied to your lawn or garden soil when temperatures are between 60°F and 70°F. The bacterium infects the gut of a Japanese beetle grub and turns it to mush. Infected grubs will have a brownish or reddish color and should be left in the soil to infect the next generation of grubs. Milky spore bacteria may remain viable in the soil for several years after application.

Treating your entire lawn can be costly and the bacteria doesn't affect adult beetles. These beetles are able to fly several miles to find sources of food, so treating your lawn won't prevent damage from adults. Use this biological pest control when grubs are causing damage to your lawn and to reduce future populations.

BENEFICIAL NEMATODES

Nematodes are tiny, unsegmented roundworms that live in the soil and feed on plants, insects, or animals, depending on the species. Dormant beneficial nematodes may be purchased at garden centers or online in a powdered form to mix with water and spray onto your garden soil or lawn.

Nematodes enter the body of a grub, caterpillar, or other insect through the mouth or another opening. It then secretes a toxic bacterium that kills the host and allows the nematode to feed on its body. There are many different species that live at different soil depths and feed on a variety of hosts. If armyworms, cutworms, Japanese beetles, root worms, or other grubs and larvae are a problem in your garden, beneficial nematodes are a safe, organic option to control them. Be sure to follow the directions on the package for the best results.

Natural Doesn't Always Mean Safe

Choosing an organic insecticide over a synthetic chemical product doesn't necessarily mean there aren't any harmful repercussions for your health or for the environment. The term "insecticide" describes a compound that kills insects, even if the compound is extracted from natural materials. Rotenone, a naturally occurring insecticide made from several species of tropical plants, is now recognized as harmful to humans and other mammals and has been implicated in the development of Parkinson's disease.

Other natural or certified organic pesticides to use with caution include (but are not limited to):

» copper sulfate
» neem oil
» nicotine
» pyrethrins (or their synthetic alternative, pyrethroids)
» sabadilla
» spinosad

Although these products are less toxic than many synthetic pesticides, they may kill beneficial insects, and the runoff from overapplication can pollute waterways and cause crustaceans, fish, and other wildlife to die. Some of these products also cause health issues for humans when they are not used properly.

20 MOST COMMON PESTS AND DISEASES

Gardening sometimes seems like a never-ending battle with insects and plant diseases. Successful gardeners are constantly on the lookout for signs of damage so they can treat the cause. Research the common pests in your area and have a plan in place if your crops are attacked. Your local extension office is a great source of information, but be aware that they adhere to Integrated Pest Management (IPM) practices that may include nonorganic measures.

Be sure to correctly identify a problem before treating it and always follow the directions on the label if using a purchased product. Here are some of the most common garden pests and diseases:

APHID

These insects are small and soft-bodied and take on a variety of colors. They suck juices from the underside of leaves and new growth on plants, and some even feed on roots. Infestations can cause leaves to turn yellow and drop off and new growth may be deformed. Ants "farm" aphids for their "honeydew" and are often an indicator of an aphid problem.

Problem for: Most plants, including fruits, herbs, ornamentals, and vegetables

How to Eradicate: A hard spray of water may dislodge aphids and knock them to the ground; spray with soapy water; or attract lady beetles and green lacewings.

ARMYWORM

The adults are small brown moths. Young caterpillars are pale green and develop brown stripes on their sides as they get older. Caterpillars feed on leaves at night and hide under foliage during the day. Infestations leave brown patches of lawn and damage to leaves of vegetable crops. Although they are more common in southern states, they do migrate north in summer.

Problem for: A variety of vegetables and fruits including beets, corn, fruit, peas, peppers, potatoes, and tomatoes

How to Eradicate: Attract parasitic wasps and ground beetles or apply *Bacillus thuringiensis* to control the caterpillar stage.

BLIGHT, EARLY

This common fungal disease appears as yellow spots that turn brown, often showing concentric circles of damage. Leaves may drop off. Brown lesions on stems may occur, and tomatoes may have brown leathery spots, whereas potato tubers may have corky spots. Fruit may be usable if damage is not severe.

Problem for: Potatoes and tomatoes

How to Eradicate: Keep leaves dry by watering at the base of plants. Leave space between plants to allow air circulation. Remove all volunteer potato plants because they may harbor the disease over winter. Remove diseased plants and throw them away instead of composting. Plant disease-resistant varieties.

BLIGHT, LATE

Irregular gray- or olive-colored lesions on leaves appear water-soaked. Leaves do not drop off, as in early blight.

Problem for: Potatoes and tomatoes

How to Eradicate: Keep leaves dry by watering at the base of plants. Leave space between plants to allow air circulation. Remove all volunteer potato plants because they may harbor the disease over winter. Remove diseased plants immediately and throw them away or bury them deeply instead of composting. Plant resistant varieties that are certified disease-free. Treat soil with *Bacillus subtilis*.

CABBAGE WORMS

There are three common species of moths that lay eggs on brassicas: cabbage looper (adult moths are mottled brown and fly at night; larvae are green with four faint white lines down the back and sides and move like an inchworm); the imported cabbage worm (adult moths are white or yellow with black spots; larvae are green with velvety skin and fine hairs, and have a light-yellow stripe down the back); and diamondback moth (adults are small, gray moths with folded wings; larvae are small and yellowish green, with a forked tail). They all create holes in leaves in a similar manner.

Problem for: Broccoli, cabbage, cauliflower, collards, kale, and other brassicas

How to Eradicate: Reduce problems by covering crops with row covers, treat plants with *Bacillus thuringiensis*, or attract predatory wasps and yellowjackets.

CLUB ROOT

This fungal disease causes swollen, oddly shaped roots on infected plants. The plant may be wilted during the day but seems to recover at night; leaves may droop and turn yellow. Plants become stunted and may die.

Problem for: Brassicas, especially cabbage; Brussels sprouts; and Chinese cabbage

How to Eradicate: Clean tools to prevent spread of fungal spores. Plant resistant varieties from a certified disease-free source. Do not plant susceptible crops in infected soil for 10 years. Planting rye as a cover crop may inhibit this disease. Clean up and destroy infected plants.

COLORADO POTATO BEETLE

The adults are oval with black-and-yellow striped wing covers. Larvae are pink to red with black spots along their sides. Eggs are light orange and found in clusters on the bottoms of host leaves. In their larval stage, Colorado potato beetles can defoliate entire plants.

Problem for: Ground cherry, nightshades, peppers, potatoes, and tomatoes

How to Eradicate: Remove all nightshade plants around the garden and clean up all garden debris. Plant varieties that produce an early crop to escape the worst damage later in the season. Handpick larvae and destroy eggs on the undersides of leaves. Attract lady beetles and stink bugs to feed on eggs. Spinosad may be used in case of severe infestations.

CORN EARWORM

The adults are buff-colored moths with irregular markings and have a wingspan of 1½ inches. Larvae are cream-colored to green and brown with stripes and small black spines along the back. Damage is found on the tip of an ear of corn first, near the base of the silk, under the husk.

Problem for: Corn and grain sorghum

How to Eradicate: Apply a few drops of mineral oil on the corn silk to prevent moths from laying their eggs in the silk. Treat with spinosad, *Bacillus thuringiensis*, or beneficial nematodes.

CUCUMBER BEETLE

Spotted and striped cucumber beetles are about ⅕ inch long and yellowish, and they have either twelve black spots or three black stripes. Their yellow eggs are found at the base of the plant. Larvae are up to ⅜ inch long and are cream-colored with a dark head. Larvae cause damage to roots and adults feed on flowers, fruits, stems, and leaves, spreading bacterial wilt and viral pathogens.

Problem for: Beans, cucumbers, cucurbits (including pumpkins, eggplants, melons, squash), and other plants.

How to Eradicate: Remove eggs and mulch around plants to prevent larvae from burrowing down to the roots. Use a row cover and remove plant debris from the garden. In severe infestations, neem oil or pyrethrins may be used.

CUTWORM

Cutworms vary in color from brown, green, or tan with stripes or plain. They curl into a C-shape and hide in the soil during the day. These nocturnal caterpillars chew through stems of small plants just above the soil level, leaving seedlings lying on the ground. The adults are medium brown or gray moths with splotches of black, blown, gray, or white.

Problem for: A wide variety of vegetable seedlings, including beans, celery, corn, lettuce, peas, peppers, and tomatoes

How to Eradicate: Surround the seedlings with cardboard collars by cutting a round section of paper towel tube and pushing it 1 to 2 inches into the soil around the plant to prevent cutworm damage. If the problem is severe, sprinkle DE or crushed eggshells around the seedlings.

FLEA BEETLE

These small beetles can be from ⅛ to ¼ inch long and vary from black, bronze, brown, or iridescent blue to metallic gray, sometimes with stripes. Their strong back legs enable them to jump like fleas, hence the name. Eggs are laid in soil, in debris, or on roots, stems, or leaves. The small white larvae feed on roots. Adult flea beetles cause damage by chewing small, irregular holes in leaves.

Problem for: A wide variety of vegetables, including cabbage, eggplant, lettuce, potatoes, radish, spinach, turnips, and many weeds.

How to Eradicate: Mulch plants to discourage larvae from burrowing into the soil to feed. Attract braconid wasps to lay their eggs on the adult female beetles. Plant radishes as a trap crop and treat with spinosad to prevent severe infestation.

GRASSHOPPER

Grasshoppers are a common pest with long, powerful hind legs, wings, and antennae that are shorter than their bodies. Nymphs (look like small adults) and adults can decimate a garden by feeding on flowers, fruits, leaves, and stems.

Problem for: Many vegetables and herbs, including carrots, lettuce, onions, and sweet corn; when grasshoppers are numerous, your entire garden is at risk.

How to Eradicate: Turn soil in the fall to kill eggs. Encourage birds, frogs, toads, and other predators to eat adult grasshoppers. Sprinkle a product containing fungal spores of *Nosema locustae* in your garden or treat plants with hot pepper spray to reduce damage.

LEAF MINER

The adults are small black flies that lay their eggs on plant leaves. The larvae feed inside the layers of leaves, showing up as squiggly discolored lines or blotches. Leaf miners can cause extensive damage to plants.

Problem for: A wide variety of garden plants, including cabbage, lettuce, peas, peppers, and spinach

How to Eradicate: Prevent infestations with row covers. Remove and destroy the infected leaves. Treat plants with *Bacillus thuringiensis* or attract parasitic wasps, such as *Diglyphus isaea*, to your garden.

MEXICAN BEAN BEETLE

This orange-to-brick-red lady beetle is one of the few species that feeds on plants instead of pests. They can be easily identified by the sixteen black spots on their wings. The larvae are orange with lines of black bristles. These pests skeletonize leaves and may cause widespread damage.

Problem for: Alfalfa, clover, cowpeas, green beans, and lima beans

How to Eradicate: Use floating row covers to prevent adults from laying eggs. Hand-pick adults and larvae; destroy eggs on the bottoms of leaves. Severe infestations may be treated with DE, neem oil, or insecticidal soap.

POWDERY MILDEW

This common fungal disease appears as a white or gray powdery fuzz on leaves, stems, and flowers. Severe problems can cause leaves to turn yellow and drop. There are many different species, each with its own host plants.

Problem for: Beans, cucumbers, melons, peas, peppers, pumpkins, squash, and tomatoes

How to Eradicate: Prevent problems by spacing plants to allow air circulation; spray with a solution of water with baking soda and dormant oil, or treat with a solution of baking soda, milk, and water (see the insecticidal soap recipe, page 58).

SQUASH BUG

Adult squash bugs are ½ inch long and gray or brown, with orange stripes on the abdomen. They lay masses of brownish eggs on the undersides of leaves. Nymphs are gray with black legs and antennae. These pests move very quickly and hide under leaves. They feed by sucking plant juices from leaves, creating yellow and brown spots and wilted plants.

Problem for: Cucumbers, gourds, melons, pumpkins, and summer and winter squash

How to Eradicate: Protect plants with row covers and check the undersides of leaves for eggs. Remove eggs and handpick nymphs and adults. Don't mulch around affected plants.

SQUASH VINE BORER

The adult moth is ½ inch long and has clear wings with black spots and a black and red body. They lay eggs at the base of plant stems, and the eggs hatch into cream-colored grubs that burrow into stems. You will most likely see wilted leaves on plants and frass (bug feces) on the stems.

Problem for: Gourds, pumpkins, summer squash, and winter squash

How to Eradicate: Protect plants with row covers or dust the base of stems with DE. If you find frass at the base of stems, cut a slit in the stem, remove the grub, then wrap the stem to protect it.

TOBACCO MOSAIC VIRUS

This virus causes yellow and green mosaic patterns on leaves, including yellow veins. Plants and leaves may be deformed and stunted.

Problem for: Beans, peppers, potatoes, tobacco, tomatoes, and many other plants

How to Eradicate: Purchase disease-free plants and seeds. Disinfect tools and hands to prevent the spread of virus. Do not use the tobacco before handling plants. Remove and throw away any affected plants.

TOMATO HORNWORM

Tomato and tobacco hornworms are large green caterpillars with white diagonal stripes on their sides and a curved "horn" on their back ends. The adults are large moths—called hawk, hummingbird, or sphinx moth—that hover over flowers like a hummingbird. The larvae can defoliate a plant quickly, leaving only the stems.

Problem for: Peppers, potatoes, tobacco, and tomatoes

How to Eradicate: Handpick hornworms. Encourage parasitic wasps that lay their eggs on hornworms. If you see a hornworm with small white capsules attached, leave them. They are eggs that will hatch into larvae that feed on the worm.

VERTICILLIUM WILT

This soilborne fungus enters the plant through the roots and quickly plugs up the vascular system, preventing water and nutrients from traveling through the plant. Leaves near the base of the plant turn yellow then brown, spreading to the top of the plant and causing the leaves to die and fall off.

Problem for: Eggplant, melons, peppers, potatoes, pumpkins, and tomatoes

How to Eradicate: Prevent problems by planting resistant varieties (V resistant) and rotating crops (do not plant in the same place for at least four years). Infected plants can't be treated and should be removed and thrown away.

CHAPTER 6

AN A TO Z OF VEGETABLES, FRUITS, AND HERBS TO GROW

When selecting vegetables, fruits, and herbs for your organic garden, you'll need to consider space, soil, and sun requirements as well as the length of your local growing season. You'll also want to know when to expect a harvest and the life cycle of your plants (see "Deciding What to Grow" on page 34).

Following are some commonly grown veggies, fruits, and herbs, along with harvesting and preserving tips. The USDA Plant Hardiness Zones are indicated for perennial crops to indicate their winter cold tolerance.

ASPARAGUS

Perennial (USDA Plant Hardiness Zones 3 to 8)

Family: Liliaceae

Seed: Sow indoors 12 weeks before last frost or plant one-year crowns outdoors as soon as soil can be worked in the spring; space plants 12 to 24 inches apart in rows 30 to 36 inches apart.

Germination Time: 14 to 56 days at temperatures of 70°F to 85°F

Time to Harvest: 3+ years after planting from seed or 2 years after planting crowns; harvest a few spears for 2 or 3 weeks from vigorous plants the year after planting healthy crowns.

How Many to Plant: Plants produce an average of ½ pound per year. Plant 10 to 20 crowns per person for fresh use in-season and some extra to preserve.

Keys to Success: Plant the asparagus in loose, deep, neutral pH soil with at least 6+ hours of sunlight per day. Fertilize with compost in spring or after harvest. Mulch heavily to prevent weeds and do not cultivate around plants to avoid damaging roots.

Potential Pests: Asparagus beetles may be handpicked. Another option is to attract lady beetles and the parasitic wasp *Tetrastichus asparagi* to control pest larvae and eggs. Fusarium crown rot and asparagus rust problems are reduced by cleaning tools, removing garden debris, and planting disease-resistant varieties such as Jersey Knight or Jersey Supreme.

When/How to Harvest: In spring, use a sharp knife to cut spears when they are 6 to 8 inches long. To preserve, blanch spears for 3 minutes in boiling water and freeze.

Helpful Hacks: Prepare beds thoroughly and add compost before planting. Dig a trench about 6 to 12 inches deep (6 to 8 inches deep if soil is heavy clay and 10 to 12 inches deep if soil is very sandy) and place the crowns so that the roots are slightly fanned out. Cover crowns with 2 to 3 inches of soil. Do not allow roots to dry out at any time before or during planting. Water the bed well after planting and keep the soil slightly moist until plants are established.

BEAN, STRING

Annual

Family: Leguminosae

Seed: Direct sow when temperatures reach 70°F to 80°F. Plant ½ to 1 inch deep and space seeds 2 to 6 inches apart and rows 24 to 36 inches apart, or 6 to 9 seeds per square foot. Thin seedlings to about 4 to 6 inches apart.

Germination Time: 4 to 10 days; speed germination by soaking seeds in water overnight.

Days to Harvest: 45 to 60 at temperatures of 60°F to 75°F

How Many to Plant: Each plant should produce about ⅒ to ¼ pound of beans. One square foot planted with 9 beans in a grid should produce close to 1 pound of beans. A 10-foot row should yield between 3 and 5 pounds.

Keys to Success: Plant the beans in well-drained, slightly acidic soil in full sunlight. Thin seedlings to 4 to 6 inches apart to allow air circulation around plants and prevent fungal disease. Plant bush beans every 2 weeks for successive harvests or plant bush beans for your first harvest and pole beans for a later harvest. Pole beans will produce over a longer period of time and will provide a larger harvest than bush beans.

Potential Pests: Aphids, Mexican bean beetles, and spider mites may be controlled by dusting leaves with DE. Anthracnose, gray mold, powdery mildew, and rust are reduced with proper spacing, cleaning tools between crops, and planting disease-resistant varieties.

When/How to Harvest: Begin harvesting when beans are about 3 inches long but before the seeds begin to fill the pod and get tough. Harvest every other day or every third day to keep plants in production. To preserve, blanch beans in boiling water for 2 to 4 minutes (small to large pods) and freeze, or pressure can.

Helpful Hacks: Plant disease-resistant varieties such as Contender or Top Crop (bush type). Try a variety of green, mottled colored beans, purple, or yellow wax for a colorful harvest.

BEET

Biennial (grown as an annual)

Family: Chenopodiaceae

Seed: Direct sow when soil may be worked in the spring. Plant ¾ inch deep and 1 inch apart in rows 12 to 24 inches apart. Thin seedlings to 3 to 6 inches apart.

Germination Time: 5 to 12 days at temperatures of 45°F to 85°F

Days to Harvest: 45 to 60

How Many to Plant: One medium beet weighs about ¼ pound. One square foot planted with 9 beets in a grid should produce 1½ to 2 pounds of roots. A 10-foot row should produce 8 to 15 pounds of beet roots. Plant a 10-foot row in spring for fresh use and a 10-foot row 10 weeks before your first frost in fall for storage beets, per person.

Keys to Success: Beets prefer well-drained, slightly acidic soil that isn't overly fertile. They prefer some shade in the middle of the day during hot weather. Each "seed" is actually composed of more than one seed, so you will need to thin the seedlings rather aggressively or the roots won't develop properly.

Potential Pests: Leaf miner may be prevented with floating row covers or by destroying infected leaves. Cercospora leaf spot and scab are reduced by irrigating with a soaker hose to prevent wet leaves more prone to fungal infections.

When/How to Harvest: Gently pull beets when they are 2 to 4 inches wide. Late-season beets keep for 2 to 5 months at 32°F to 40°F and 90 to 95 percent humidity.

Helpful Hacks: Bull's Blood is a disease-resistant heirloom variety great for greens. Cylindra is another heirloom red beet with a long, cylindrical root. Golden (yellow root) and Albino (white root) beets are sweeter and milder in flavor than red beets.

BROCCOLI

Biennial (grown as an annual)

Family: Brassicaceae

Seed: Sow indoors 6 to 11 weeks before last frost and transplant to garden or cold frame at 4 to 6 weeks old, or direct sow ½ inch deep as soon as the soil can be worked in spring. Plant seedlings 18 to 24 inches apart in rows 24 to 30 inches apart.

Germination Time: 4 to 7 days at 45°F to 85°F

Days to Harvest: 55 to 75 from transplanting

How Many to Plant: One plant should produce ¾ to 1 pound of broccoli in an 18-to-24-by-18-to-24-inch space. A 10-foot row should produce 4 to 6 pounds of broccoli. Plant a 10-foot row in early spring and a 10-foot row in late summer to have fresh broccoli and preserve some for later.

Keys to Success: Plant broccoli in deep, rich, neutral soil in full sunlight. Broccoli bolts (flowers) when temperatures reach 80°F, so plant early enough to harvest before the summer heat sets in. Do not cultivate around plants to prevent damage to shallow roots. Keep the soil moist.

Potential Pests: Cabbage root worms, cabbage worms, and flea beetles may be prevented with floating row covers or by treating with DE. Reduce clubroot and heat rot by growing broccoli where no other brassicas have grown for at least 3 to 5 years.

When/How to Harvest: Use a sharp knife to cut the broccoli stem below the head when the florets are fully formed, before they turn yellow and begin to flower. To preserve, blanch broccoli florets in boiling water for 3 minutes and freeze.

Helpful Hacks: The varieties Valiant and Everest are resistant to head rot. Try planting heirlooms that produce many small florets over a long period of time instead of one large head, such as Calabrese or Purple Sprouting broccoli varieties.

BRUSSELS SPROUTS

Biennial (grown as an annual)

Family: Brassicaceae

Seed: Sow indoors 3 to 4 weeks before last frost and transplant to the garden when the danger of frost is minimal. Direct seed in areas with a long growing season. In southern areas, plant 10 to 14 weeks before the first fall frost, and in frost-free areas, plant in October to harvest in late winter. Space plants 18 inches apart in rows 24 to 30 inches apart.

Germination Time: 5 to 8 days at temperatures of 45°F to 85°F

Days to Harvest: 65 to 90 from transplanting

How Many to Plant: Each plant should produce 2 to 3 pounds of Brussels sprouts. A 10-foot row should produce 14 to 22 pounds of sprouts. Plant about 5 plants per person for fresh use and some to preserve.

Keys to Success: Plant Brussels sprouts in deep, rich, neutral soil with 6+ hours of full sunlight. Do not cultivate around plants to prevent damage to shallow roots. Keep soil moist. Side-dress seedlings with plenty of compost.

Potential Pests: Cabbage root worms, cabbage worms, and flea beetles may be prevented with floating row covers or treating with DE. Reduce clubroot fungus by growing Brussels sprouts where no other brassicas have grown for at least 3 to 5 years.

When/How to Harvest: Twist sprouts from the stem when they are 1½ to 2 inches in diameter. The flavor is much sweeter after a frost. Remove yellowing leaves from the bottom of the plant up as you harvest to direct energy to sprout production. To preserve, blanch for 3 to 5 minutes (small to large sprouts) and freeze.

Helpful Hacks: For gardeners with a short growing season, try Tasty Nuggets Brussels sprouts for an early harvest. If space is at a premium, Long Island and Long Island Improved have a compact growth habit. Dominator and Icarus take longer to produce but are more disease-resistant.

CABBAGE

Biennial (grown as an annual)

Family: Brassicaceae

Seed: Start indoors 4 to 6 weeks before the last frost and transplant to the garden after the last frost, or direct seed in areas with a long growing season. In frost-free areas, plant cabbages in late August or September for winter harvest. Plant seeds ½ inch deep and space plants 12 to 18 inches apart and rows 24 to 30 inches apart.

Germination Time: 3 to 7 days at temperatures of 45°F to 85°F

Days to Harvest: 70 to 110 (depending on variety)

How Many to Plant: One plant should produce a 1½- to 4-pound head of cabbage. A 10-foot row should produce 7 to 10 cabbages with a weight of 10 to 40 pounds. Plant about 5 early season cabbages in spring and 5 to 10 late-season cabbages in late summer per person for fresh use and preserving.

Keys to Success: Plant in deep, rich, neutral pH soil with 6+ hours of full sunlight. Do not cultivate around plants to prevent damage to shallow roots. Keep soil evenly moist and side-dress seedlings with extra compost.

Potential Pests: Cabbage root worms, cabbage worms, and flea beetles may be prevented with floating row covers or treat with DE. Reduce black rot and clubroot fungus by growing cabbage where no other brassicas have grown for at least 3 to 5 years.

When/How to Harvest: Cut through the stem below the head when the cabbage forms a firm head. You may also cut the cabbage into small wedges, blanch in boiling water for 1½ minutes, and freeze. You may also store cabbages (with roots intact) at 32°F to 40°F and 95 percent humidity for up to 4 months.

Helpful Hacks: Early Jersey Wakefield and Golden Acre are early-maturing heirloom varieties with some disease-resistance. Danish Ballhead has a longer growing season than other varieties and keeps well in winter.

CARROT

Biennial (grown as an annual)

Family: Apiaceae

Seed: Direct sow 2 to 3 weeks before the last frost. Sow ½ inch deep and ½ inch apart in rows 12 to 24 inches apart. Thin seedlings to 2 to 4 inches apart by cutting the tops off unwanted plants.

Germination Time: 7 to 21 days at temperatures of 50°F to 85°F

Days to Harvest: 60 to 80

How Many to Plant: One square foot planted with 16 carrots should produce 2 to 4 pounds of roots. A 10-foot row should produce 5 to 10 pounds. Plant a 10-foot row per person for enough carrots for fresh use and preserving.

Keys to Success: Carrots need deep, sandy soil free from stones with a neutral to slight acidic pH. Plant in full sunlight. Do not fertilize with nitrogen or the leaves will grow at the expense of roots. Carrots can take a long time to germinate, and the soil must be kept moist or the sprouting seeds will die.

Potential Pests: Carrot rust maggots may be prevented with a floating row cover. This cover also prevents leafhoppers from spreading aster yellows disease, which causes bitter, hairy roots.

When/How to Harvest: Baby carrots may be harvested to thin the row. Harvest your main crop after a light frost for sweetest flavor. To preserve, cut carrots into ¼-inch slices, blanch in boiling water for 2 minutes, and freeze. You may also pressure can carrots or store unwashed carrots (with greens removed and root kept intact) at 32°F to 40°F and 95 percent humidity for up to 6 months.

Helpful Hacks: For small spaces, try planting small varieties such as Thumbelina or Little Finger. For a late-season crop, plant a variety that keeps well, such as Nantes or Chantenay. Gardeners with heavy soil will have better luck with short, blocky varieties, such as Danvers Half Long, Nantes, or Chantenay.

CORN, SWEET

Annual

Family: Gramineae

Seed: Direct sow after all danger of frost has passed. Plant seeds 1 inch deep and 6 to 12 inches apart in rows 12 to 36 inches apart. Plant at least 4 rows together for proper pollination.

Germination Time: 4 to 7 days at temperatures of 65°F to 85°F

Days to Harvest: 60 to 100

How Many to Plant: Each plant should produce 1 or 2 ears of corn. A 4-by-4-foot block of 16 cornstalks planted in a grid should produce 16 to 32 ears. Plant a 4-by-4-foot block of sweet corn per person to provide enough for fresh use with extra to preserve for later.

Keys to Success: Plant in full sunlight and well-drained, fertile soil with plenty of compost and a slightly acidic pH. Be sure to sow the seeds in 4-by-4 or larger blocks to ensure pollination and kernel development. Side-dress with compost after seedlings emerge. Isolate different varieties to prevent cross-pollination that can cause poor flavor.

Potential Pests: Plant early to deter corn earworm. Clean up cornstalks in fall to prevent European corn borers from overwintering in garden. Avoid watering leaves to prevent rust and, to reduce future problems, remove corn smut galls before they release spores.

When/How to Harvest: Harvest when silks begin drying out and kernels near the center of the ear are full-size and have a milky-colored juice. To preserve, blanch whole ears in boiling water for 7 to 11 minutes and kernels for 4 minutes, then freeze. Sweet corn may also be pressure canned.

Helpful Hacks: Check the seed packet to determine if the sweet corn variety is Sugary (SU: sweet, grows well in cooler conditions, doesn't last long), Supersweet (SH2: very sweet, somewhat picky about growing conditions, lasts 1 week in the refrigerator), or Sugar Extended (SE: very sweet, picky about growing conditions, lasts 1 week in the refrigerator). Some hybrids are labeled "triple sweet" and are the result of breeding SE and SH2 varieties. For disease-resistance, try hybrid varieties such as Silver Queen. Heirloom varieties that produce a good crop include Country Gentleman and Golden Bantam.

CUCUMBER

Annual

Family: Cucurbitaceae

Seed: Sow indoors 3 to 4 weeks before last frost and transplant to the garden after all danger of frost is gone, or direct sow in similar fashion. Sow 1 to 1½ inches deep, 2 inches apart in hills (3 to 5 feet apart) or rows (5 to 6 feet apart). Thin seedlings to 8 inches apart.

Germination Time: 3 to 10 days at temperatures of 60°F to 90°F

Days to Harvest: 50 to 70

How Many to Plant: Each full-size plant should produce 4 to 6 pounds of cucumbers (bush plants produce less). Grow 2 to 4 plants per person for fresh use and preserving.

Keys to Success: Plant in well-drained, fertile soil with a slightly acidic pH in a spot with 6+ hours of sunlight. Work plenty of compost into the soil and mulch with compost. Keep the soil evenly moist and harvest cucumbers every other day to keep the plants in production. To avoid spreading disease, do not handle the plants when they are wet.

Potential Pests: Prevent squash vine borer and cucumber beetles with floating row covers. Cucumber beetles spread bacterial wilt. Powdery mildew and cucumber mosaic virus problems may be reduced by planting resistant varieties, increasing air circulation, and by cleaning up garden debris.

When/How to Harvest: Harvest cucumbers when they reach the desired size, before they start turning yellow, by cutting the stem to avoid damaging the plant. Cucumbers are best preserved by pickling. They may also be sliced and dehydrated as "chips."

Helpful Hacks: Disease-resistant heirloom varieties include Armenian, Lemon, and Northern Pickling. For small spaces, choose a bush variety such as Patio Pickle or Bushy.

EGGPLANT

Tender perennial (grown as an annual in temperate zones)

Family: Solanaceae

Seed: Start indoors 8 to 10 weeks before last frost. Transplant to garden when nighttime temperature is 50°F or warmer. Sow ¼ inch deep and plant seedlings 18 to 24 inches apart in rows 30 to 36 inches apart. Direct seed when nighttime temperatures are 50°F or warmer in areas with a long growing season.

Germination Time: 7 to 14 days at temperatures of 60°F to 95°F

Days to Harvest: 60 to 80 from transplanting

How Many to Plant: Each plant should produce 3 to 6 pounds of eggplant. Grow 4 to 6 plants per person for fresh use and preserving.

Keys to Success: Plant in well-drained, fertile soil with a neutral pH, in a spot with 6+ hours of full sunlight. Do not overfertilize with nitrogen or the plants will grow foliage at the expense of fruit. Mulch with compost and do not cultivate close to plants to avoid damaging roots.

Potential Pests: Prevent cutworm damage with cardboard collars around seedlings. Reduce flea beetle damage by sprinkling DE around base of plant early in season. Do not plant eggplants where tomatoes and potatoes have grown over the past 3 years.

When/How to Harvest: Harvest eggplants with garden shears when the skin is still glossy and the fruit is firm. Do not leave the fruit on the plant once the skin loses its glossy sheen, or the yield will diminish. To preserve: peel and slice eggplants ½ inch thick and blanch in boiling water with lemon juice (1 gallon of water to ½ cup lemon juice to prevent browning of fruit), and freeze.

Helpful Hacks: Black Beauty is a popular heirloom variety that produces large, purple fruits. Disease-resistant varieties to try include Diamond (large, purple), Ping Tung Long (heirloom; long, slender, purple), and Rosa Bianca (heirloom; medium, lavender).

GARLIC

Perennial (USDA zones 4 to 9)

Family: Alliaceae

Plant: Plant 1 to 3 weeks after your first frost in the Fall. Plant cloves 3 inches deep and 6 inches apart, in double or triple rows, 6 inches apart, to save space. Mulch with straw over winter.

Time to Harvest: 1 year from planting

How Many to Plant: Each clove will produce 1 bulb of garlic. One square foot planted with 9 garlic cloves in a grid will provide 9 garlic bulbs with a total average weight of about 1 pound. A 10-foot row should produce 25 to 30 bulbs, enough for a small family to use fresh and preserve.

Keys to Success: Plant in well-drained, fertile soil with plenty of compost mixed in. Choose a spot with 6+ hours of full sunlight. Space cloves 4 to 6 inches apart and mulch well. Cut garlic flower buds (scapes) when they are small so the plant will direct energy to clove production instead of flowers. Use scapes in place of garlic in cooking.

Potential Pests: If onion maggots are a problem, cover plants with a floating row cover to deter them. Prevent fusarium basal rot by planting disease-free cloves, keeping the beds weeded, and being careful not to damage the roots when cultivating.

When/How to Harvest: Harvest garlic when the lower leaves turn brown. Dig up a bulb and check it. If the bulb fills its papery hull, your garlic is ready to harvest. Allow the garlic bulb to cure for 3 to 4 weeks in a warm, dry spot with good air ventilation. To preserve: peel the garlic and freeze without blanching or store up to 6 months (hardneck varieties) or up to 9 months (softneck varieties) at 32°F to 40°F and 50 to 60 percent humidity.

Helpful Hacks: Hardneck garlic varieties are relatively cold hardy, easier to peel, and produce larger cloves and a central reproductive stalk (scape). Elephant garlic is a common hardneck variety. Softneck varieties do best in milder climates, have tighter "skins" with smaller cloves, and usually do not produce a scape. Softneck garlic can keep for 9 months, whereas hardneck varieties must be used or frozen in 4 to 6 months. California Softneck is a common softneck variety.

KALE

Biennial (grown as an annual)

Family: Brassicaceae

Seed: Start indoors up to 3 months before the last frost and transplant to the garden up to 6 weeks before the last frost or direct seed as soon as the soil can be worked in spring. Plant a fall crop in midsummer. Sow ¼ to ½ inch deep and thin to 8 to 12 inches apart with rows 18 to 30 inches apart.

Germination Time: 4 to 7 days at temperatures of 40°F to 80°F

Days to Harvest: 45 to 75

How Many to Plant: Each plant should produce about ¼ pound of greens. Plant 8 or more plants per person for fresh use in-season. Plant a fall crop to harvest well into winter.

Keys to Success: Plant in well-drained, fertile soil with neutral pH in full sunlight or in a spot with light shade during the heat of day. Keep soil evenly moist and side-dress with compost several times during season. In mild climates, you may harvest kale all winter.

Potential Pests: Cabbage loopers, cabbage worms, cutworms, and slugs are common. Do not plant where other brassicas have grown for at least 3 years to prevent fungal disease such as club root.

When/How to Harvest: Harvest baby kale when leaves are 3 inches or larger, or allow the plants to mature and pick large outer leaves, leaving the crown to continue production for an extended harvest. To preserve, blanch kale in boiling water for 2 minutes, then freeze or dehydrate.

Helpful Hacks: Red Russian kale is a very cold hardy variety and may be harvested all winter in milder growing zones. Lacinato kale, or "Dinosaur" kale, is a popular variety for cooking. Winterbor and Vates are cold hardy, productive, and resistant to disease and pests, making them an excellent choice for home gardens.

LETTUCE, LEAF

Annual

Family: Asteraceae

Seed: Start indoors 3 to 4 weeks before transplanting or direct sow as soon as the soil can be worked in spring until 2 to 3 weeks before last frost. Plant seeds ⅛ to ¼ inch deep, and thin to 4 to 10 inches apart with rows 12 to 18 inches apart. Seedlings are cold hardy and may be moved outside several weeks before your last frost in spring.

Germination Time: 4 to 7 days at temperatures of 40°F to 70°F

Days to Harvest: 30 to 85

How Many to Plant: Each plant should produce about ½ pound of greens. One square foot with 9 plants should produce 4 to 5 pounds of lettuce. A 10-foot row should produce 12 to 16 pounds of lettuce. Plant 6 to 10 plants every 2 weeks per person in spring and 6 to 10 plants in mid-to-late summer for fall harvest.

Keys to Success: Plant in well-drained, fertile soil with plenty of compost and a slightly acidic pH in part shade to full sunlight. Shade will keep lettuce from bolting as quickly in hot weather. Sow in a cold frame for early harvest and sow every 2 weeks until 2 to 3 weeks before the last frost in spring for an extended harvest in spring and early summer. Plant again 45 to 60 days before the first frost in fall for a late-season crop.

Potential Pests: Prevent slugs and snails with slug bait or DE. Protect seedlings from cutworms with cardboard collars. Protect lettuce with floating row covers to keep leaf miners from damaging leaves and reduce problems with aster yellows, a disease spread by leafhoppers.

When/How to Harvest: Harvest leaf lettuce at any stage of growth. Use baby lettuce in salads after thinning rows. Extend harvest by removing outer leaves when they are large and allow small inner leaves to continue producing, or cut the entire plant, leaving a 2- to 3-inch base to regrow another harvest of lettuce. Lettuce doesn't store well.

Helpful Hacks: Plant heat-resistant varieties of lettuce to extend your harvest into early summer. Black Seeded Simpson, Cimmaron Romaine, Oakleaf, and Slobolt varieties are slower to bolt in summer.

ONION, STORAGE

Biennial (grown as an annual)

Family: Alliaceae

Seed: Sow indoors 8 to 10 weeks before last frost or direct seed when soil reaches 50°F. Sow seeds ¼ inch deep, 1 inch apart in rows spaced 12 to 18 inches apart. Start indoors or purchase onion sets for short growing seasons. In areas with long growing seasons, storage onions may be direct seeded. Thin them to 3 to 4 inches apart.

Germination Time: 4 to 5 days at temperatures of 45°F to 95°F

Days to Harvest: 100 to 175

How Many to Plant: Storage onions should produce 4 to 5 pounds per square foot planted in a 3-by-3 grid or 20 to 30 pounds per 10-foot single row. Plant a 10-foot row for winter storage for a small family.

Keys to Success: Plant in well-drained soil with plenty of compost mixed in and a neutral-to-slightly-acidic pH in full sunlight. Keep beds well weeded, keep soil evenly watered, and do not overfertilize with nitrogen.

Potential Pests: Onion maggot and purple blotch problems may be controlled by rotating crops and removing garden debris.

When/How to Harvest: Harvest storage onions when about half of the tops fall over and dry out. Cure them between 75°F and 90°F in a well-ventilated area for 2 to 4 weeks until the outer scales dry out and the necks tighten. Store onions for 4 to 6 months at 32°F to 50°F and 60 to 70 percent humidity.

Helpful Hacks: Storage onions are categorized by day length needed for bulb formation. Short-day onions are sweeter and form bulbs with 10 to 12 hours of sunlight. Vidalia is one of the most popular varieties. Long-day varieties need 14 to 16 hours of sunlight to form bulbs and store for 4 to 6 months. Consider raising Brunswick, Copra, or Yellow Sweet Spanish for storage.

PEAS

Annual

Family: Leguminosae

Seed: Direct sow into the garden as soon as the soil can be worked, in spring or midsummer for a fall harvest. Plant as a winter crop in warm climates. Sow 1 to 1½ inches deep and 2 to 4 inches apart in rows 18 to 24 inches apart. Thin to 4 inches apart.

Germination Time: 7 to 21 days at temperatures of 40°F to 85°F

Days to Harvest: 50 to 70

How Many to Plant: One square foot with 9 plants in a grid should produce about 1 cup of shelled peas. A 10-foot row should produce 3 to 4 pounds. Snow peas are more productive because the plants are not directing energy into seed production. Harvest shoots and leaves for salads. Raise a 10- to 20-foot row per person to eat fresh and preserve a few extras.

Keys to Success: Plant in well-drained soil with a neutral pH in full sunlight. Mulch to keep weeds down and keep soil evenly moist. Plant along a trellis to support vines and save space. Bush varieties also benefit from a small fence or other support.

Potential Pests: Protect plants from aphids and cutworms with DE. Reduce problems with fungal diseases such as wilt and powdery mildew by cleaning debris from the garden in fall.

When/How to Harvest: Gently twist snow peas from the vine before the peas begin to fill the pod. Harvest shelling peas when the pods are full but before they begin to yellow. To preserve, blanch shelled peas in boiling water for 1½ minutes and freeze.

Helpful Hacks: Plant disease-resistant varieties such as Cascadia, Frosty, or Lincoln if fungal diseases are a problem in your garden. For snow peas, Oregon Sugar Pod and Oregon Giant both produce large, tender pea pods.

PEPPER, BELL

Tender perennial

Family: Solanaceae

Seed: Start indoors 8 to 12 weeks before the last frost or direct seed in areas with long growing season. Sow ¼ inch deep. Transplant to the garden when nighttime temperatures are 55°F or warmer. Plant peppers 12 to 24 inches apart in rows 24 to 30 inches apart.

Germination Time: 7 to 10 days at temperatures of 70°F to 95°F

Days to Harvest: 60 to 150 from transplanting

How Many to Plant: Each bell pepper plant should produce 3 to 4 pounds of green peppers and somewhat less if peppers are allowed to ripen to orange, purple, red, or yellow. In areas with a long growing season, you may harvest 5 pounds or more from productive plants.

Keys to Success: Plant in well-drained soil with a slightly acidic pH in full sunlight. Don't rush to transplant peppers to your garden in the spring. Cool temperatures will delay fruit production. You may need to stake larger plants to prevent the weight of the fruit breaking their branches.

Potential Pests: Tomato hornworms may be handpicked. Prevent cutworm damage with cardboard collars. Do not plant peppers where ground cherries, eggplant, potatoes, or tomatoes were grown in the previous 3 years to reduce diseases such as bacterial canker, early blight, and verticillium wilt.

When/How to Harvest: Bell peppers may be harvested when they reach full size, either as a green pepper or wait for the fruit to ripen to their mature color of red, yellow, orange, or purple. To increase harvests, pick the first 2 or 3 peppers when they are green. Doing so signals the plant to increase fruit production. To preserve, halve or slice peppers, seed, and freeze without blanching, or dehydrate.

Helpful Hacks: Consider raising peppers in a container and bring them indoors over the winter to keep them as a perennial. Try raising mini bell peppers or sweet banana peppers for an earlier harvest.

POTATO

Annual

Family: Solanaceae

Plant: Plant potato sets in the garden after soil temperatures are 40°F or warmer. Cut seed potatoes into chunks with at least one "eye" per set. Allow cut potatoes to cure for several days in a humid location with temperatures of 50°F to 65°F before planting. Plant potato sets 4 inches deep and 8 to 12 inches apart in rows 24 to 36 inches apart.

Sprouting Time: 14 to 21 days

Days to Harvest: 60 to 90

How Many to Plant: Each plant will grow in a space of about 1 square foot and should produce about 2 pounds of potatoes. For each pound of seed potatoes planted, you should harvest around 10 pounds of potatoes. A 10-foot row planted with 10 to 15 potato sets should produce 10 to 40 pounds of potatoes.

Keys to Success: Plant in well-drained soil with low-nitrogen compost mixed in with an acidic pH in full sunlight. Hill potatoes when plants reach 6 to 8 inches tall and again every 2 weeks until the plants begin to die back. Plants produce more potatoes along stems that are covered with soil.

Potential Pests: Colorado potato beetles may be prevented from laying eggs

on plants by protecting with floating row cover, or by handpicking larvae. Floating row covers will also prevent or reduce damage from aphids, flea beetles, and leafhoppers. Prevent scab, early blight, and late blight by planting potatoes where no other nightshade plants have been grown for at least 3 years.

When/How to Harvest: When plants start flowering, small potatoes are beginning to form underground. Wait several weeks after flowering to begin harvesting new potatoes for fresh use. Harvest potatoes for storage after the tops of the plants turn brown and die back. Potatoes keep for 4 to 6 months at 36°F to 40°F and 90 percent humidity.

Helpful Hacks: Varieties good for storage include Burbank Russet, Elba, Katahdin, Red Pontiac, and Yukon Gold. If fungal diseases are a problem in your garden, consider resistant varieties such as Dark Red Norland, Kennebec, Lehigh, and Rose Finn Apple.

PUMPKIN / WINTER SQUASH

Annual

Family: Cucurbitaceae

Seed: Sow indoors 2 to 3 weeks before your last frost in areas with short growing seasons or direct seed in areas with long growing seasons. Transplant seedlings to the garden or direct seed 2 to 3 weeks after the last frost, when the temperatures are 70°F during the day. Sow 1 to 1½ inches deep with 4 to 5 seeds per hill and space hills 5 to 8 feet apart. Thin seedlings to 2 to 3 plants per hill.

Germination Time: 5 to 10 days at temperatures of 60°F to 105°F

Days to Harvest: 85 to 110

How Many to Plant: Expect 2 to 5 fruits per plant, 4 to 15 fruits per hill. Mini pumpkins and small varieties of winter squash may be more prolific. Plant 1 hill or more per person for winter storage.

Keys to Success: Plant in well-drained, fertile, slightly acidic soil in full sunlight. Mix in plenty of compost and keep the soil evenly moist. Mulch to suppress weeds unless slugs, snails, and squash bugs are a problem.

Potential Pests: Control squash bugs and squash vine borers with floating row cover until plants begin to flower, then remove the cover to allow pollination.

Control slugs and snails with slug bait or DE. To prevent spread of fungal disease, do not plant pumpkins or winter squash in areas where cucurbits (cucumbers, gourds, melons, pumpkins, and squash) have been planted for at least 3 years.

When/How to Harvest: Harvest before a hard frost. Cut the stem several inches from the fruit and allow the pumpkins and squash to cure in the garden for 1 to 2 weeks or move the fruits to a warm spot indoors to cure. To preserve, cook, peel, seed, and mash pumpkins and winter squash, then freeze. Pumpkins keep 1 to 2 months and some winter squash varieties keep 5 to 6 months at 50°F to 55°F and 50 to 70 percent humidity.

Helpful Hacks: Plant disease-resistant pumpkin varieties such as Baby Bear, Howden, and Jack-Be-Little. Disease-resistant varieties of winter squash include Bush Delicata, Spaghetti, and Sugar Dumpling. Consider planting Bush Delicata squash, Bushkin pumpkin, and Pilgrim butternut squash in small spaces.

SPINACH

Annual

Family: Chenopodiaceae

Seed: Direct sow in the garden as soon as the soil can be worked in spring. Sow seeds ½ inch deep and 1 inch apart in rows 12 to 18 inches apart. Thin seedlings to 2 to 3 inches apart. Plant again in late summer through fall for a late harvest. In areas with hot summers and mild winters, plant spinach in fall, winter, and early spring.

Germination Time: 6 to 21 days at temperatures of 40°F to 75°F

Days to Harvest: 35 to 45

How Many to Plant: One square foot with 9 plants in a grid should produce ⅓ to 1 pound of greens and a 10-foot row should provide about 4 pounds of spinach. Plant 1 square foot of spinach every 1 to 2 weeks for enough fresh greens per person or a 10-foot row every week to 2 weeks during spring and again in late summer to provide fresh greens and spinach for preserving per person.

Keys to Success: Plant in well-drained, fertile soil with plenty of compost and slightly-acidic-to-slightly-alkaline soil with full sunlight or part shade. Spinach benefits from shade in the hot part of the day to prevent early bolting. Side-dress with compost and keep the soil evenly moist. Spinach stressed from crowding, underwatering, or heat will bolt.

Potential Pests: Flea beetles and leaf miners are deterred with a floating row cover. Slugs and snails may be controlled with slug bait or DE. Problems with anthracnose, damping off, and root rot are reduced by rotating crops, cleaning up garden debris, and watering plants with drip irrigation to prevent wetting the leaves.

When/How to Harvest: Begin cutting baby spinach as soon as the leaves are large enough to use. Continue harvesting leaves as they mature, until the plant begins to bolt, or cut the entire plant when the leaves reach a usable size. To preserve, blanch spinach for 1 to 2 minutes and freeze.

Helpful Hacks: If various fungal diseases are a problem in your garden, plant resistant varieties such as Acadia, Bloomsdale Long Standing, Giant Noble, and Winter Bloomsdale. Consider planting bolt-resistant varieties such as Correnta, Spinner, and Tyee for an extended harvest.

SQUASH, ZUCCHINI AND SUMMER

Annual

Family: Cucurbitaceae

Seed: Sow indoors 2 to 3 weeks before your last frost or direct sow after all danger of frost. Sow ½ to 1 inch deep and 4 inches apart in rows 4 to 5 feet apart. Thin seedlings to 12 to 24 inches apart.

Germination Time: 5 to 10 days at temperatures of 60°F to 105°F

Days to Harvest: 45 to 60

How Many to Plant: One summer squash or zucchini plant needs about 4 square feet of space and should produce 5 to 12 pounds of squash. A 10-foot row should produce 25 to 75 pounds of squash. Plant 1 or 2 plants per person for fresh use and some to preserve.

Keys to Success: Plant in well-drained, fertile soil with plenty of compost and a slightly acidic pH in full sunlight. Side-dress seedlings with compost and mulch to retain moisture and keep weeds down.

Potential Pests: Squash bugs and squash vine borer are deterred with a floating row cover, but the cover must be removed for pollination when plants begin to flower. Reduce fungal disease by rotating crops, planting when soil has warmed, provide ample space between plants for air circulation, and water plants with drip irrigation to prevent wetting the leaves.

When/How to Harvest: Use a sharp knife to cut zucchini and summer squash from the vine when they are 6 to 12 inches long for tender squash. Squash grows quickly and should be checked daily. To preserve, slice squash ½ inch thick and blanch in boiling water for 3 minutes then freeze.

Helpful Hacks: Try several different varieties of summer squash such as Bennings Green Tint scalloped, Black Beauty zucchini, Cocozelle, Ronde de Nice, or Yellow Zebra.

TOMATO

Annual

Family: Solanaceae

Seed: Sow indoors 6 to 8 weeks before last frost or direct seed in areas with long seasons. Sow ⅛ inch deep. Transplant seedlings to the garden after all danger of frost and when temperatures remain above 45°F at night. Space seedlings 12 to 24 inches apart, depending on their mature size.

Germination Time: 6 to 12 days at temperatures of 60°F to 95°F

Days to Harvest: 60 to 90

How Many to Plant: Determinate varieties are smaller, set all their fruit in a short time, and should produce between 2 and 8 pounds of fruit per plant. Indeterminate varieties can produce 10 pounds or more over several weeks. A 10-foot row should produce a harvest of 20 to 50 pounds. Raise 2 or 3 plants per person for fresh use and a 10-foot row per person for enough to preserve.

Keys to Success: Plant in well-drained soil with a moderate amount of compost mixed in and slightly-acidic-to-neutral pH in full sunlight. Stake and mulch the plant to reduce fungal disease on leaves.

Potential Pests: Handpick hornworms. Keep soil evenly moist to reduce problems with blossom end rot. Do not plant tomatoes where other nightshades have grown over the past 3 years.

When/How to Harvest: Twist each tomato from the vine when it is almost fully ripe, or harvest when the color just begins to change if they are prone to damage from pests. As long as tomatoes have started coloring up, they will ripen in a sunny windowsill. To preserve: peel, seed, and freeze without blanching.

Helpful Hacks: Choose determinate varieties if space is limited, or plant indeterminate varieties for larger harvests. Paste tomatoes have less moisture and are best for preserving. Cherry, grape, and salad tomatoes are good for snacking and salads. Beefsteak tomatoes are great for slicing. Consider Black Cherry or Sungold for fresh eating. Roma makes good sauce and Brandywine is one of the best slicing tomatoes.

BLACKBERRY AND RASPBERRY

Woody perennial (USDA zones 3 to 10)

Family: Rosaceae

Plant: Plant disease-free bramble roots in early spring, setting roots 1 inch deeper than they were planted in nursery pots. Place roots 30 to 36 inches apart with rows 10 feet apart.

Germination Time: N/A (not usually planted from seed)

Time to Harvest: 3 months to 2 years from planting

How Many to Plant: One plant should produce 1 to 2 quarts of berries and a 10-foot row of brambles should provide 3 to 8 quarts of berries. Plant a 10-foot row per person for fresh eating and a 20-foot row per person for enough to preserve.

Keys to Success: Plant in well-drained, sandy soil with a slightly acidic pH and full sunlight. Locating brambles along a fence allows gardeners to tie the canes up, making harvest, pruning, and care easier to manage. Mulch brambles with compost to keep weeds under control. There are two main growth habits for bramble fruits: floricanes and primocanes. Floricanes produce fruit from buds on second-year canes, then die back over winter. Primocanes produce fruit at the ends of first-year canes in the fall of the year they are planted, and again on the lower part of the same cane in the summer of the following year.

Potential Pests: Japanese beetles can destroy leaves and fruit. Handpick or use a Japanese beetle trap as far from plantings as possible to trap and kill adults. Apply beneficial nematodes or milky spore to turf and garden areas to control larvae. Reduce fungal disease problems by cleaning up infected leaves and canes, and by planting disease-resistant varieties.

When/How to Harvest: Harvest berries when they turn color and pull from stems easily. Use berries quickly because they don't store well. To preserve, freeze berries whole, make freezer jam, or can jam in a hot water bath canner.

Helpful Hacks: Plant disease-resistant varieties such as Crimson Night and Double Gold raspberries or Navaho thornless blackberry.

BLUEBERRY

Woody perennial (USDA zones 3 to 10)

Family: Ericaceae

Plant: Plant 2- to 3-year-old bareroot blueberries in spring and potted blueberries in spring or fall. Space plants 4 to 5 feet apart in rows 10 feet apart.

Germination Time: N/A (not usually planted from seed)

Time to Harvest: 3 to 4 years

How Many to Plant: One plant should produce 3 to 10 pounds. Plant 2 or 3 blueberry bushes per person for fresh use and preserving.

Keys to Success: Plant in well-drained, fertile soil with an acidic pH in full sunlight. Keep soil evenly moist. Mulch around plants to control weeds. Blueberries are self-fruitful but will produce a larger harvest with cross-pollination.

Potential Pests: Blueberry maggots can ruin berries. Coat berries with kaolin clay mixed with water and a few drops of dish soap to act as a barrier. Clean up leaves and dead berries under the plants to reduce problems with fungal disease.

When/How to Harvest: Harvest berries when they are fully colored and sweet. Berries will keep on the plant for a few

days, but birds can pick them clean if they are left too long. To preserve, freeze berries whole, make freezer jam, or can jam in a hot water bath canner.

Helpful Hacks: Blueberry varieties belong to one of the following groups: lowbush (short, winter hardy), northern highbush (tall, winter hardy), southern highbush (medium, grows well in southern states), half-high (medium, hardiest varieties, bred from lowbush and highbush types), and rabbiteye (tall, best for mild and warm climates). Some good cultivars for home gardens include Blueray, Elliot, Misty, and Patriot.

GRAPE

Woody perennial (USDA zones 3 to 10)

Family: Vitaceae

Plant: Plant bareroot or potted plants at the same depth as they were planted in pot (2 to 3 inches above root level) as soon as soil can be worked in spring. Space plants 8 to 10 feet apart in rows 8 feet apart.

Germination Time: N/A (not usually planted from seed)

Time to Harvest: 2 to 3 years from planting

How Many to Plant: One plant should produce 10 to 20 pounds of fruit. Plant 1 or 2 vines per person (2 or more if you choose a variety that is not self-fruitful) for fresh use and preserving.

Keys to Success: Plant in well-drained soil with a slightly acidic pH in full sunlight. In northern areas, plant vines on a south-facing slope if possible. Train grapes on an arbor, fence, or trellis to keep vines and fruit off the ground. Grapes need good air circulation and plenty of sun for the best fruit. Mulch with compost.

Potential Pests: Japanese beetles and grape berry moths can destroy harvests. Place a Japanese beetle trap as far as possible from the garden to trap adults, or use beneficial nematodes or milky spore to control larvae. Reduce damage from grape berry moths and fungal diseases, such as black rot, botrytis, and powdery mildew by cleaning up dropped berries and infected leaves.

When/How to Harvest: Harvest grapes when they are fully colored and sweet. The sugar content will not increase after harvest. Cut bunches of grapes with sharp pruners or shears. Pulling them from the vine may damage the plant. To preserve: freeze seedless grapes whole, press the grapes and freeze the juice, or can in water bath container.

Helpful Hacks: Choose hardy disease-resistant varieties and prepare their site in advance. Varieties for northern growers include Concord and King of the North. In southern areas, choose a variety of muscadine grape, such as Delicious or Dixie.

MELON

Annual

Family: Cucurbitaceae

Seed: Sow indoors 2 to 4 weeks before last frost, or direct seed in areas with a long growing season. Sow ½ inch deep with 3 to 4 seeds in hills set 4 to 6 feet apart or 12 inches apart in rows set 4 to 5 feet apart. Thin seedlings to 2 to 3 per hill or 12 to 24 inches apart in rows.

Germination Time: 3 to 10 days at temperatures of 60°F to 95°F

Days to Harvest: 70 to 100

How Many to Plant: Each plant should produce 2 to 5 melons. Plant 2 or 3 plants per person for fresh use.

Keys to Success: Plant in well-drained, fertile, and somewhat acidic soil in full sunlight. Keep soil evenly moist and mulch heavily with compost. In areas with short growing seasons, allow each vine to set 3 or 4 fruits and remove additional female flowers to direct energy to ripening fruit. Do not overwater or the fruit may crack and rot. Cantaloupe, honeydew, and watermelon are the most common melons grown.

Potential Pests: Aphids, cucumber beetles, flea beetles, squash bug, and squash vine borer are deterred with a floating row cover, or handpick larger pests. Prevent fungal diseases, such as bacterial wilt, fusarium wilt, and powdery mildew by cleaning up garden debris in fall, allowing good air circulation, rotating the crops, and planting resistant varieties.

When/How to Harvest: As they ripen, the bottoms of melons will change from green to a creamy or yellow color. Cantaloupes smell fragrant and the stem will pull away from the melon easily. Watermelons sound hollow when thumped. The rind of honeydew will turn to a creamy yellow when ripe. If pests are a problem, you may harvest a few days early to prevent damage to ripening melons. To preserve: peel, cut melons into cubes, and freeze.

Helpful Hacks: If fungal disease is an issue in your garden, consider choosing a resistant variety, such as Athena hybrid (cantaloupe), Crimson Sweet heirloom (watermelon), and Honey Star hybrid (honeydew). Gardeners with small spaces may grow compact varieties such as Cal Sweet Bush watermelon or Minnesota Midget cantaloupe.

STRAWBERRY

Herbaceous perennial (USDA zones 3 to 9)

Family: Rosaceae

Plant: Plant strawberries in spring. Bareroot plants should be situated so the crown is just above ground level. Potted plants should be planted at the same depth as they were in the pot. Plant June-bearing strawberries 18 to 24 inches apart in rows 4 feet apart. Plant ever-bearing and day-neutral varieties 8 to 12 inches apart in rows 12 inches apart.

Germination Time: N/A (not usually planted from seed)

Time to Harvest: Most varieties are ready to harvest the second year after planting.

How Many to Plant: June-bearing strawberries produce 1 to 2 pounds of fruit per plant. Everbearing and day-neutral varieties produce about 1 pound per plant from spring through fall. Plant 10 to 20 June-bearing strawberries per person to provide enough fruit for fresh use and preserving.

Keys to Success: Plant in well-drained, fertile soil with a slightly acidic pH and full sunlight. Mulch plants with straw to prevent weeds and hold moisture. To prevent injury to the plants, do not cultivate around the shallow roots.

Potential Pests: Tarnished plant bug and strawberry bud weevil can cause damage to fruit. Use a floating row cover to reduce problems and treat heavily infested plants with pyrethrin or sabadilla as a last resort. Floating row covers will also prevent damage from birds; however, cover plants after flowers are pollinated. Verticillium wilt is reduced by planting strawberries in a bed where tomatoes and other nightshades (alternate hosts) have not been grown in 3 or more years.

When/How to Harvest: Pick berries when they have ripened and the end of berries turn red. If birds or other creatures steal the berries, you may pick them a day early to reduce loss. Berries do not ripen once they are picked. To preserve, freeze berries whole, make freezer jam, or can jam in a hot water bath canner.

Helpful Hacks: Plant a selection of early-, mid-, and late-season June-bearing varieties hardy in your area for an extended harvest of berries in spring. Consider planting day-neutral or everbearing varieties for smaller harvests from late spring through fall.

BASIL

Annual

Family: Lamiaceae

Seed: Sow indoors 6 to 8 weeks before the last frost in spring or direct sow after all danger of frost. Sow ¼ inch deep and 1 to 2 inches apart. Thin or transplant seedlings to 6 to 12 inches apart.

Germination Time: 5 to 7 days at temperatures of 70°F to 85°F

Days to Harvest: 50 to 60

How Many to Plant: Each plant should produce around ½ pound of leaves per season. Raise 2 or 3 plants to produce enough fresh basil per person and 6 to 8 plants to produce extra for drying.

Keys to Success: Plant in well-drained soil with plenty of compost and a neutral pH with full sunlight. Side-dress plants with compost to reduce weeds and increase fertility. Pollinators enjoy basil nectar, so consider allowing some plants to flower.

Potential Pests: Handpick Japanese beetles. Use slug bait or DE dusted around the base of plants to prevent damage from slugs and snails. If aphids become problematic, attract lady beetles and green lacewings to the garden or spray plants with insecticidal soap in the early morning to avoid spraying pollinators.

When/How to Harvest: Begin harvesting leaves when plants have at least 6 sets of leaves. Pinch the growing ends of stems to prevent flowering for a longer harvest of tender leaves. Alternatively, you may grow basil as a microgreen crop. To preserve, dehydrate extra basil or chop, mix with butter or vegetable oil, and freeze in small portions.

Helpful Hacks: Try growing a selection of basil varieties for their unique flavors. Sweet basil is commonly grown for culinary use. Lettuce leaf basil has large, mild flavored leaves that are a tasty alternative to lettuce. Other favorites include Dark Opal, Holy, Lemon, Lime, and Thai basil, which make delicious additions to your garden.

CHIVES

Herbaceous perennial (USDA zones 3 to 10)

Family: Alliaceae

Seed: Sow indoors 10 to 12 weeks before your last frost, or direct seed in the garden as soon as soil can be worked in spring. Sow ¼ to ½ inch deep and space plants 1 to 2 inches apart. Seeds need darkness to germinate. You may also plant divisions in early spring or fall.

Germination Time: 14 to 21 days at temperatures of 60°F to 80°F

Days to Harvest: 60+ from seeds, or 30+ from transplanting

How Many to Plant: One plant should produce 2 or 3 cups of chopped chives per year once it is established. Plant 1 or 2 bunches per person for fresh use and preserve the extras for later.

Keys to Success: Plant in well-drained soil with plenty of compost mixed in and a slightly-acidic-to-neutral pH in full sunlight. Mulch around established plants to reduce weeds. Keep soil evenly moist. Divide plants every few years by digging the clump, cutting into 3 or 4 sections, and replanting the divisions in a newly prepared bed. Chives are a great plant for beneficial insects, so allow them to produce flowers.

Potential Pests: Chives have few problems with pests and disease. Thrips can cause damage and look similar to little black flies. Infestations may be avoided by crushing these pests with your fingers when first detected. If the problem persists, spray with homemade garlic spray (see page 59) or insecticidal soap (see page 58) early in the morning to avoid spraying on pollinators.

When/How to Harvest: Cut leaves near the base when they are still young and tender. Do not harvest more than one-third of the plant at a time. To preserve, dehydrate extra chives or chop, mix with butter or vegetable oil, and freeze in small portions.

Helpful Hacks: Try growing garlic chives for a different flavor.

CILANTRO

Annual

Family: Apiaceae

Seed: Direct sow in the garden as soon as the soil can be worked in spring. Sow every 2 to 3 weeks for continued harvests through the season. Sow seeds ¼ inch deep and 2 to 3 inches apart in rows 12 inches apart. Thin seedlings to every 6 to 8 inches apart.

Germination Time: 7 to 10 days at temperatures of 55°F to 70°F

Days to Harvest: 21 to 30

How Many to Plant: One plant should produce about ¼ cup of fresh cilantro or 1 tablespoon of coriander seeds. Plant about 6 plants per person every 2 to 3 weeks until the weather warms for fresh cilantro and for dried coriander seeds.

Keys to Success: Plant in well-drained soil with plenty of compost and a slightly acidic pH in part shade to full sunlight. In areas where the temperatures increase quickly in late spring, a partly shaded spot delays bolting. Cilantro flowers attract beneficial insects, so consider planting extras and allowing them to flower and produce coriander seeds for winter cooking.

Potential Pests: Cilantro has few pest and disease problems. Aphids can be controlled by attracting lady beetles and green lacewings to the garden or spraying with insecticidal soap (see page 58) in the early morning to avoid spraying on beneficial insects.

When/How to Harvest: Harvest upper leaves of cilantro any time before they become tough. To harvest coriander seeds, wait until they are brown and crack when you squeeze them. Dry seeds indoors before storing. To preserve, dehydrate extra cilantro or use in water bath–safe canning recipes for salsa.

Helpful Hacks: Try an improved variety of cilantro, such as Slow-bolt, for longer harvests.

DILL

Annual

Family: Apiaceae

Plant: Direct sow in the garden after the last frost. Sow ¼ inch deep and 2 to 4 inches apart in rows 24 inches apart. Thin seedlings to 10 to 12 inches apart. Dill doesn't transplant well.

Germination Time: 10 to 14 days at temperatures of 60°F to 70°F

Days to Harvest: 40 to 90

How Many to Plant: Each plant should produce around ¼ pound of greens and 3 to 5 tablespoons of seed. Plant 3 or 4 plants per person for fresh use and preserving.

Keys to Success: Plant in well-drained soil with plenty of compost mixed in and a slightly acidic pH in full sunlight. Side-dress seedlings with compost and keep soil evenly moist. Dill flowers attract many beneficial insects, and swallowtail butterflies lay their eggs on these plants.

Potential Pests: Aphids can spread viral infections as they feed on dill. To reduce problems, plant dill in a spot where carrots have not grown for at least 3 years.

Remove infested leaves and plants that show stunted growth.

When/How to Harvest: You may begin harvesting dill leaf when the plants are 6 to 8 inches tall. Flowers may be used in pickling, or leave them to develop seed. Harvest seeds when they begin turning brown and dry them completely indoors to store for later. To preserve, dehydrate dill leaf and seed, or use in pickling recipes.

Helpful Hacks: For small spaces, try a compact variety of dill, such as Fernleaf, which is also slow to flower. Mammoth is a large variety with good flavor, and Bouquet produces a lot of seeds for pickling and culinary use.

PARSLEY

Biennial (grown as an annual)

Family: Apiaceae

Plant: Sow indoors 6 to 8 weeks before your last frost, or direct sow in the garden. Soak seeds in warm water overnight and sow ⅛ inch deep and 3 to 4 inches apart in rows 24 to 30 inches apart. Thin seedlings to 10 to 12 inches apart.

Germination Time: 14 to 30 days at temperatures of 65°F to 85°F

Days to Harvest: 70 to 90

How Many to Plant: One plant should produce between ¼ and ½ pound over the course of the growing season. Plant 2 or 3 plants per person for fresh use and 4 to 6 plants for fresh use and preserving.

Keys to Success: Plant in well-drained soil with plenty of compost mixed in and slightly acidic soil in full sunlight. Keep seeds and plants evenly moist and side-dress seedlings with compost. Parsley is a host plant for swallowtail butterflies, so consider planting extra for these pollinators.

Potential Pests: Leafhoppers spread aster yellows disease. Prevent these pests by covering parsley with floating row cover. Plant parsley in a spot where carrots and celery have not grown for at least 3 years.

When/How to Harvest: You may begin harvesting parsley when the plants are 4 to 6 inches tall. Harvest by picking the entire stem. Removing just the leaves reduces production. To preserve, dehydrate extra parsley or chop, mix with butter or vegetable oil, and freeze in small portions.

Helpful Hacks: There are curly and flat-leaf varieties of parsley. The flat-leaf varieties are more productive and just as tasty as curly varieties. Consider planting a disease-resistant variety such as Paramount.

SAGE

Perennial (USDA zones 5 to 8)

Family: Lamiaceae

Plant: Sow seeds indoors, direct sow in garden, or plant potted sage in the garden. Soak seeds in warm water overnight and sow ⅛ inch deep and 2 to 3 inches apart. Thin seedlings to 18 to 24 inches apart.

Germination Time: 7 to 21 days at temperatures of 65°F to 80°F

Days to Harvest: 75 to 100

How Many to Plant: One mature sage plant should produce ½ pound of fresh leaves or more per season. One or 2 plants should produce enough for fresh use and drying for most families.

Keys to Success: Plant in sandy, well-drained soil with a slightly acidic pH in full sunlight. Sage does not tolerate wet soil. Prune new growth back by several inches once or twice each growing season to prevent leggy growth. Sage tends to be a short-lived perennial, so you may wish to start new plants when the old ones begin to get woody.

Potential Pests: Sage is susceptible to root rot in wet soils. There are very few pests that cause serious damage, but slugs and aphids may cause a decline in health. Use slug bait and attract lady beetles and green lacewings to keep pests under control.

When/How to Harvest: You may begin pinching off a few leaves for fresh use once the plant is 6 to 8 inches tall. At the end of the growing season, harvest green, healthy leaves to dehydrate for winter. To preserve, dehydrate extra sage or chop, mix with butter or vegetable oil, and freeze in small portions.

Helpful Hacks: There are a number of different varieties of sage, including golden, purple, and tricolor. Some varieties are less hardy, so check before planting.

APPENDIX

30 INSECTARY PLANTS TO PROTECT YOUR GARDEN

Choose insectary plants native to your area that do well in your growing conditions. Make sure a species is not invasive before adding it to your garden. Plant a diversity of plants from different families, to reduce problems with pests and disease.

COMMON NAME/ BOTANICAL NAME	PLANT FAMILY	PLANT TYPE	USDA ZONE	INSECT(S) IT ATTRACTS
Allium *Allium tanguticum*	Amaryllidaceae	Perennial	4 – 10	hoverflies, Braconid wasps, Ichneumonid wasps, and Trichogramma wasps
Alyssum, Basket of Gold *Aurinia saxatilis*	Brassicaceae	Perennial	3 – 8	lady beetles, hoverflies
Butter and Eggs *Linaria vulgaris*	Plantaginaceae	Perennial	3 – 9	hoverflies, Braconid wasps, Ichneumonid wasps, and Trichogramma wasps
California Buckwheat *Eriogonum fasciculatum*	Polygonaceae	Perennial	7 – 11	lady beetles, hoverflies, tachinid flies

→

COMMON NAME/ BOTANICAL NAME	PLANT FAMILY	PLANT TYPE	USDA ZONE	INSECT(S) IT ATTRACTS
Caraway *Carum carvi*	Apiaceae	Biennial	4 – 10	ground beetles, big-eyed bugs, damsel bugs, minute pirate bugs, hoverflies, lacewings, Braconid wasps, Ichneumonid wasps, Trichogramma wasps
Carpet Bugleweed *Ajuga reptans*	Lamiaceae	Perennial	3 – 10	lady beetles, hoverflies
Cilantro/Coriander *Coriandrum sativum*	Apiaceae	Annual	N/A	lady beetles, hoverflies, lacewings, Braconid wasps, Ichneumonid wasps, and Trichogramma wasps
Cinquefoil, Alpine *Potentilla villosa*	Rosaceae	Perennial	3 – 7	lady beetles, hoverflies, Braconid wasps, Ichneumonid wasps, and Trichogramma wasps
Cinquefoil, Sulfur *Potentilla recta*	Rosaceae	Perennial	3 – 8	lady beetles, hoverflies, Braconid wasps, Ichneumonid wasps, and Trichogramma wasps
Cosmos *Cosmos bipinnatus*	Asteraceae	Annual	N/A	big-eyed bugs, damsel bugs, minute pirate bugs, hoverflies, lacewings, Braconid wasps, Ichneumonid wasps, Trichogramma wasps
Dill *Anethum graveolens*	Apiaceae	Annual	N/A	ground beetles, lady beetles, hoverflies, lacewings, Braconid wasps, Ichneumonid wasps, Trichogramma wasps
Fennel *Foeniculum vulgare*	Apiaceae	Perennial	4 – 9	ground beetles, lady beetles, big-eyed bugs, damsel bugs, minute pirate bugs, hoverflies, lacewings, Braconid wasps, Ichneumonid wasps, Trichogramma wasps

COMMON NAME/ BOTANICAL NAME	PLANT FAMILY	PLANT TYPE	USDA ZONE	INSECT(S) IT ATTRACTS
Four-Wing Saltbush *Atriplex canescens*	Amaranthaceae	Perennial	3 – 11	lady beetles, hoverflies, lacewings
Golden Marguerite *Anthemis tinctoria*	Asteraceae	Perennial	3 – 8	lady beetles, hoverflies, tachinid flies, Braconid wasps, Ichneumonid wasps, Trichogramma wasps
Goldenrod *Solidago* species	Asteraceae	Perennial	3 – 8	big-eyed bugs, damsel bugs, minute pirate bugs, hoverflies
Lemon Balm *Melissa officinalis*	Lamiaceae	Perennial	4 – 9	hoverflies, tachinid flies, Braconid wasps, Ichneumonid wasps, and Trichogramma wasps
Marigold, Signet *Tagetes tenuifolia*	Asteraceae	Annual	N/A	big-eyed bugs, damsel bugs, minute pirate bugs, ground beetles, lady beetles, hoverflies, Braconid wasps, Ichneumonid wasps, and Trichogramma wasps
Masterwort *Astrantia major*	Apiaceae	Perennial	4 – 7	hoverflies, Braconid wasps, Ichneumonid wasps, and Trichogramma wasps
Parsley *Petroselinum crispum*	Apiaceae	Biennial	5 – 8	hoverflies, tachinid flies, Braconid wasps, Ichneumonid wasps, and Trichogramma wasps
Pennyroyal *Mentha pulegium*	Lamiaceae	Perennial	5 – 9	hoverflies, tachinid flies, Braconid wasps, Ichneumonid wasps, Trichogramma wasps
Purple Poppy Mallow *Callirhoe involucrata*	Malvaceae	Perennial	4 – 8	hoverflies, lacewings, Braconid wasps, Ichneumonid wasps, Trichogramma wasps

⟶

COMMON NAME/ BOTANICAL NAME	PLANT FAMILY	PLANT TYPE	USDA ZONE	INSECT(S) IT ATTRACTS
Queen Anne's Lace *Daucus carota*	Apiaceae	Biennial	3 - 9	lady beetles, lacewings, Braconid wasps, Ichneumonid wasps, Trichogramma wasps
Spearmint *Mentha spicata*	Lamiaceae	Perennial	4 - 10	big-eyed bugs, damsel bugs, minute pirate bugs, hoverflies
Speedwell, Spike *Veronica spicata*	Plantaginaceae	Perennial	3 - 8	lady beetles, hoverflies
Stonecrop, Orange *Sedum kamtschaticum*	Crassulaceae	Perennial	2 - 9	hoverflies, Braconid wasps, Ichneumonid wasps, Trichogramma wasps
Tansy *Tanacetum vulgare*	Asteraceae	Perennial	4 - 8	lady beetles, lacewings, tachinid flies, Braconid wasps, Ichneumonid wasps, Trichogramma wasps
Thyme, Crimson *Thymus serpyllum coccineus*	Lamiaceae	Perennial	4 - 9	hoverflies, tachinid flies, Braconid wasps, Ichneumonid wasps, Trichogramma wasps
Yarrow, Common *Achillea millefolium*	Asteraceae	Perennial	3 - 9	lady beetles, hoverflies, Braconid wasps, Ichneumonid wasps, Trichogramma wasps
Yarrow, Fern-Leaf *Achillea filipendulina*	Asteraceae	Perennial	3 - 10	ground beetles, lady beetles, assassin bugs, big-eyed bugs, hoverflies, lacewings, Braconid wasps, Ichneumonid wasps, Trichogramma wasps
Zinnia, Common *Zinnia elegans*	Asteraceae	Annual	N/A	hoverflies, Braconid wasps, Ichneumonid wasps, Trichogramma wasps

30 EASY-CARE POLLINATOR PLANTS

Choose a variety of different pollinator plants, including species native to your area, to attract myriad colorful butterflies, bees, and other pollinators to your garden. Remember to select your plants from different plant families, to reduce problems with pests and disease.

COMMON NAME/ BOTANICAL NAME	PLANT FAMILY	PLANT TYPE	USDA ZONE	POLLINATOR(S) IT ATTRACTS
Alyssum, Sweet *Lobularia maritima*	Brassicaceae	Annual	N/A	bees, butterfly larvae, butterflies
Anise Hyssop *Agastache foeniculum*	Lamiaceae	Perennial (Short-lived)	4 - 9	bees, butterflies, hummingbirds
Aster *Symphyotrichum* species	Asteraceae	Perennial	3 - 8	bees, butterflies
Bee Balm *Monarda* species	Lamiaceae	Perennial	3 - 9	bees, butterflies, hummingbirds
Borage *Borago officinalis*	Boraginaceae	Annual	N/A	bees, butterfly larvae
Butterfly Bush *Buddleja davidii*	Scrophulariaceae	Perennial	5 - 9	bees, butterflies, hummingbirds
Calendula *Calendula officinalis*	Asteraceae	Annual	N/A	bees, butterflies
Cardinal Flower *Lobelia cardinalis*	Campanulaceae	Perennial	1 - 10	bees, butterflies, hummingbirds

→

COMMON NAME/ BOTANICAL NAME	PLANT FAMILY	PLANT TYPE	USDA ZONE	POLLINATOR(S) IT ATTRACTS
Daylily *Hemerocallis*	Asphodelaceae	Perennial	4 - 9	bees, butterflies, hummingbirds
Delphinium *Delphinium elatum*	Ranunculaceae	Perennial	3 - 7	bees, butterflies, hummingbirds
Four O'Clocks *Mirabilis jalapa*	Nyctaginaceae	Perennial (Tender)	7 - 10	bees, hummingbirds
Foxglove *Digitalis*	Plantaginaceae	Biennial	4 - 10	bees, butterflies, hummingbirds
Geranium, Hardy *Geranium*	Geraniaceae	Perennial	4 - 8	bees, butterflies
Globe Thistle *Echinops sphaerocephalus*	Asteraceae	Perennial	3 - 9	bees, butterflies, hummingbirds
Hollyhock *Alcea rosea*	Malvaceae	Biennial	3 - 8	bees, butterfly larvae, butterflies, hummingbirds
Joe-Pye Weed *Eutrochium purpureum*	Asteraceae	Perennial	4 - 9	bees, butterflies, hummingbirds
Lavender *Lavandula angustifolia*	Lamiaceae	Perennial	5 - 9	bees, butterflies, hummingbirds
Liatris *Liatris spicata*	Asteraceae	Perennial	3 - 8	bees, butterflies, hummingbirds
Lupine *Lupinus*	Leguminosae	Perennial (Short-lived)	4 - 8	bees, butterfly larvae, butterflies, hummingbirds
Milkweed *Asclepias*	Apocynaceae	Perennial	4 - 9	bees, butterfly larvae, butterflies, hummingbirds

COMMON NAME/ BOTANICAL NAME	PLANT FAMILY	PLANT TYPE	USDA ZONE	POLLINATOR(S) IT ATTRACTS
Musk Mallow *Malva moschata*	Malvaceae	Perennial	3 - 8	bees, butterflies, hummingbirds
Northern Spicebush *Lindera benzoin*	Lauraceae	Perennial Shrub	4 - 9	bees, butterfly larvae, butterflies hummingbirds
Oregano *Origanum vulgare*	Lamiaceae	Perennial	5 - 12	bees, butterflies
Phlox *Phlox paniculata*	Polemoniaceae	Perennial	4 - 8	bees, butterflies, hummingbirds
Purple Coneflower *Echinacea*	Asteraceae	Perennial	3 - 9	bees, butterflies, hummingbirds
Sage *Salvia officinalis*	Lamiaceae	Perennial	5 - 8	bees, butterflies, hummingbirds
Scabiosa *Scabiosa*	Caprifoliaceae	Perennial (Short-lived)	5 - 9	bees, butterflies, hummingbirds
Shasta Daisy *Leucanthemum*	Asteraceae	Perennial	4 - 9	bees, butterflies, hummingbirds
Verbena *Verbena officinalis*	Verbenaceae	Perennial (Tender)	6 - 10	bees, butterflies, hummingbirds
Willow *Salix*	Salicaceae	Woody Perennial	4 - 10	bees, butterfly larvae, butterflies

USDA PLANT HARDINESS MAP

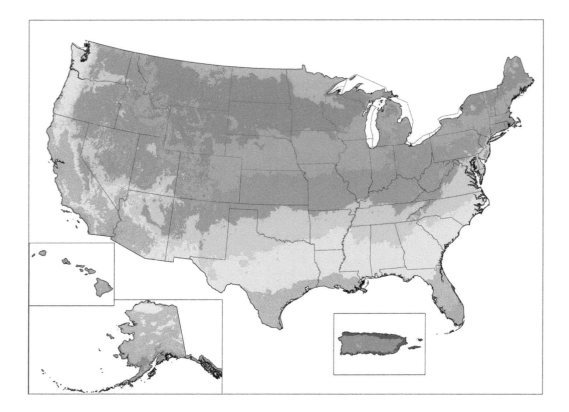

ZONE - AVERAGE ANNUAL LOW

1: -60°F to -50°F

2: -50°F to -40°F

3: -40°F to -30°F

4: -30°F to -20°F

5: -20°F to -10°F

6: -10°F to 0°F

7: 0°F to 10°F

8: 10°F to 20°F

9: 20°F to 30°F

10: 30°F to 40°F

11: 40°F to 50°F

12: 50°F to 60°F

13: 60°F to 70°F

Source: USDA Plant Hardiness Zone Map: Average Annual Extreme Minimum Tempurature 1976-2005.

GLOSSARY

Aeration: incorporation of air pockets into soil, reducing compaction and improving soil structure.

Amendment: organic material worked into the soil to adjust pH and improve structure and nutrient content for plant growth.

Annual: a plant that completes its entire life cycle within one year.

Biennial: a plant that produces vegetative growth in the first year, then flowers and sets seed in its second year.

Broadcast: to scatter seeds or fertilizer over a broad area.

Clay: tiny, platelike soil particles that are easily compacted, preventing proper water drainage. The smallest of the three types of soil particles.

Companion planting: pairing two or more crops that grow well together for a variety of reasons such as pest-repelling qualities, compatible nutrient needs, or efficient use of garden space.

Composting: the process of breaking down organic material into a nutrient-rich amendment that feeds soil microbes and increases plant growth.

Crop rotation: the practice of planting a series of different plants, or plant families, in a space to prevent the depletion of soil nutrients and problems with pests and disease.

Fungi: organisms that feed on organic matter and reproduce by the dispersal of spores, including molds, mushrooms, toadstools, and yeasts.

Hyphae: a branching, rootlike filament of the mycelium of a fungus.

Insectary plants: plants grown to provide food, shelter, or habitat for predatory or parasitic insects that feed on garden pests.

Legume: a plant from the family Leguminosae that forms root nodules around nitrogen-fixing bacteria in the soil. The bacteria convert atmospheric nitrogen into a form easily absorbed by plant roots.

Loam: soil that has balanced proportions of the three types of soil particles: clay, sand, and silt. Loam is the most sought-after soil type for gardening because it allows for proper drainage while retaining minerals and nutrients important for plant growth.

Macronutrients: the three elements necessary in greatest quantities for plant growth: nitrogen, phosphorous, and potassium.

Microbes: microscopic organisms (life-forms), such as bacteria and yeast.

Micronutrients: the seven essential elements necessary in small quantities for healthy plant growth: boron, chlorine, copper, iron, manganese, molybdenum, and zinc.

Mulch: material applied as a layer on top of soil in gardens and landscaping to prevent weeds, increase fertility, hold in moisture, or provide a more attractive appearance.

Mycelium: the mass of rootlike hyphae that make up the vegetative body of a fungus or fungus-like bacterial colony.

Perennial: a plant that lives for three or more years. This term is usually applied to herbaceous perennials that die back to the ground in winter in temperate zones. However, woody plants such as trees and shrubs are classified as woody perennials.

Permaculture: an agricultural system modeled after sustainable ecosystems from nature into a self-sustaining means of food production.

pH: the measure of acidity and alkalinity on the pH scale ranging from 0 (strongly acidic) to 14 (strongly alkaline), with 7 being neutral.

Rhizosphere: the thin layer of soil surrounding plant roots where the chemistry and microbiology is influenced by plant secretions, respiration, and nutrient exchange between the plant and soil microbes.

Sand: large, coarse soil particles that allow for the rapid drainage of water and leaching of soil nutrients. The largest of the three types of soil particles.

Silt: granular soil particles originating from quartz and feldspar. Silt particles are medium in size compared with sand and clay particles.

Succession planting: raising several crops, one after the other, in the same space. Sow staggered plantings of the same crop every two or three weeks, or plant different crops in the same space to take advantage of optimal growing conditions throughout the season.

Thinning: removing seedlings or plants to allow for proper spacing between the remaining plants. Thinning is best accomplished by cutting or pinching the stem rather than pulling up the roots, which may damage surrounding plants.

Tilling: turning over or working the soil to kill weeds and prepare for planting a crop.

RESOURCES

50+ Free Raised Bed Garden Plans and Ideas That Are Easy to Build
Epic Gardening, EpicGardening.com/raised-bed-garden-plans

All You Need to Know About Keyhole Gardening
Bob Vila, BobVila.com/articles/keyhole-gardening

Attracting Pollinators to Your Garden Using Native Plants
U.S. Forest Service (USDA), FS.Fed.us/wildflowers/pollinators/documents
/AttractingPollinatorsV5.pdf

Basic Food Preservation Information
National Center for Home Food Preservation, NCHFP.UGA.edu

Find Your Average First and Last Frost Dates by Zip Code
The Old Farmer's Almanac, Almanac.com/gardening/frostdates

A Gardener's Guide to Soil Testing
North Carolina State Extension, Content.CES.NCSU.edu/a-gardeners-guide
-to-soil-testing

How Much Soil Do I Need? Calculate the Amount of Soil You Need for Your Raised Bed or Planter
Gardener's Supply, Gardeners.com/how-to/soil-calculator/7558.html

How to Build a DIY Trellis
This Old House, ThisOldHouse.com/landscaping/21016691/how-to
-build-a-trellis

Organic 101: Five Steps to Organic Certification
USDA, USDA.gov/media/blog/2012/10/10/organic-101-five-steps
-organic-certification

Plant Disease Identification Guides
GrowVeg, GrowVeg.com/plant-diseases/us-and-canada

REFERENCES

"Crystalline Silica." National Cancer Institute at the National Institutes of Health. Last updated Feb. 1, 2019. Cancer.gov/about-cancer/causes-prevention/risk/substances/crystalline-silica.

Karavina, Charles, Ronald Mandumbu, Emmanuel Zivenge, and Tonderai Munetsi. "Use of Garlic (*Allium sativum*) as a Repellent Crop to Control Diamondback Moth (*Plutella xylostella*) in Cabbages (*Brassica oleraceae* var. *capitata*)." *Journal of Agricultural Research* 52, no. 4 (Feb. 2015): 615–621.

INDEX

ACKNOWLEDGMENTS

Many thanks to my editor, Gurvinder Gandu, for guiding me through the creative process and to Callisto Media for the opportunity to share my love of organic gardening with the world.

Special thanks to my dad, for helping me plant my first packet of seeds and to my mom, for teaching me how to preserve the harvest from our garden. Thank you to my siblings Beth, Lance, and Colleen, for helping make gardening a lot more fun, way back when we were kids.

Most of all, thank you to my husband, Tom, and my son, Joe, for encouraging me to grow and dream.

ABOUT THE AUTHOR

Lisa Lombardo is the author of *The Beginner's Guide to Backyard Homesteading*. She earned an associate's degree in applied science in landscape design and a bachelor degree in fine arts. She worked in horticulture and landscape design before becoming a full-time gardener, homesteader, blogger, and author. Growing up on a homestead with livestock and a large garden influenced her to raise her own food on urban, suburban, and rural lots for more than 30 years.

Lisa shares her knowledge and adventures at The Self Sufficient HomeAcre and The New Homesteader's Almanac and has contributed articles to various websites. She lives outside of Chicago with her family and a menagerie of pets and poultry.

CPSIA information can be obtained
at www.ICGtesting.com
Printed in the USA
BVHW051718081121
620888BV00005B/5